D0236531

THE BRITISH MUSEUM
Illustrated Encyclopaedia of

Contents

Trails

Follow an Egyptian trail!
To help you find your way around the Encyclopaedia, there are a number of 'trails' to follow.

This is how to follow a trail:
Look at the headings on these two pages and decide which topic you are most interested in. Let's say you want to follow the trail that will lead you to information on Myth and Magic… Under 'Myth and Magic' you'll find a list of words or terms. For each of these there's an entry in the Encyclopaedia that's related to your chosen topic. The entries are in alphabetical order throughout the book, so it should be easy to find the ones you want. Look up the items in the list – each will tell you something different about Myth and Magic.

Every trail is identified by its own little icon. This icon is the one that will help you spot all the Myth and Magic entries.

If you prefer, you can just browse through the Encyclopaedia and look out for the Myth and Magic icon as you turn over the pages. Whenever you see this icon under a title, you know that the entry below contains information on Myth and Magic.

All the trails can be followed in the same way. Happy hunting!

Other ways to find information:
■ Throughout the book you'll see words and terms picked out in **bold** type. Each of the topics highlighted in this way has its own separate entry in the Encyclopaedia, which you can look up alphabetically.

■ If you can't find something in the alphabetical entries, try the Index on page 174.

Everyday Life

Follow this trail to learn about Egyptian life – where people lived, what they ate, drank and wore, and how they got along together.

Children
Clothes
Crime and punishment
Education
Family
Food and drink
Furniture
Government
Houses
Law and order
Society
Towns
Trade
Women

The Natural World

Follow this trail to find out more about the ancient Egyptians' relationship with the natural world.

Animals
Birds
Egypt
Fish and fishing
Flowers
Gardens
Hunting
Oasis
Sacred animals
Snakes
Trees

Making Things

Follow this trail to learn about how the ancient Egyptians made the beautiful objects found in their homes and tombs.

Art
Cartonnage
Faience
Glass
Gold
Jewellery
Linen
Metals
Painting and drawing
Papyrus
Pots
Sculpture
Stone

Work

Follow this trail to learn about different occupations in Egypt.

Army
Building
Doctors and medicine
Farming
Fish and fishing
Hunting
Metals
Priests and priestesses
Scribes
Servants
Slaves
Stone
Temples
Trade

Leisure

Follow this trail to find out how the ancient Egyptians enjoyed their free time.

Dance
Festivals
Jokes
Music
Sports
Stories
Toys and games

Death and the Afterlife

Follow this trail to find out what the Egyptians did when somebody died and what they believed about life after death.

Abydos
Afterlife
Anubis
Book of the Dead
Canopic jars
Cemeteries
Coffins
Funerals
Mummies
Osiris
Pyramids
Tombs
Underworld Books
Ushabti
Valley of the Kings
Valley of the Queens

Kings and Queens

Follow this trail to find out about the lives of Egypt's most famous rulers.

Akhenaten
Amenhotep III
Cleopatra VII
Hatshepsut
Khufu
Nefertari
Nefertiti
Ptolemy
Rameses II
Rameses III
Senusret III
Sneferu
Thutmose III
Tutankhamun
Zoser

Egypt and its Neighbours

Follow this trail to discover more about Egypt's place in the ancient world.

Army
Diplomacy
Egypt
Egypt's neighbours
Greeks
Israel and Judah
Nubia
Romans
Trade
Travel
Warfare

Gods and Goddesses

Follow this trail to find out about the gods and goddesses of Egypt.

Amun
Anubis
Bastet
Bes
Hathor
Horus
Isis
Khnum
Maat
Min
Neith
Nephthys
Nut
Osiris
Ptah
Ra
Sekhmet
Seth
Sobek
Thoth
Two Ladies

Bible Links

Follow this trail to explore the connections between Egypt and the Bible.

Copts
Israel and Judah
Joseph
Late Period
Moses
Third Intermediate Period

Myth and Magic

Follow this trail to read stories about Egyptian gods and goddesses and discover how their symbols were used in magic.

Amulets
Apophis
Bes
Creation myths
Eye of Horus
Eye of Ra
Isis
Magic
Scarab
Sekhmet
Serqet
Snakes
Taweret
Thoth
Underworld Books
Uraeus

A Abu Simbel

The great pharaoh **Rameses II** was as famous for his huge building schemes as for his military adventures, and wherever he conquered territory he made sure to leave plenty of massive statues and monuments to impress the local people and remind them of his power. In **Nubia**, to the south of Egypt, he had two **temples** carved into a cliff at Abu Simbel.

The bigger temple was dedicated to Rameses himself. Outside are four enormous seated statues of the king, each over 20 m (60 ft) high. Inside, reliefs telling the story of Rameses' battle against the Hittites (see **Egypt's neighbours**) at Qadesh were carved on the walls as a warning to any Nubians who might have been thinking of rebelling against Egyptian rule. Rameses wanted to make sure his Nubian subjects knew he was divine. At the very back of the temple, the sanctuary contains a statue of him as a god alongside figures of the gods **Ra**, **Ptah** and **Amun**. Twice a year the rising sun shines right into the sanctuary, lighting up the statues.

The smaller temple was built for Rameses' favourite wife, **Nefertari**, and is dedicated to the goddess **Hathor**. The front is covered with statues of Rameses and Nefertari surrounded by their children. Inside, reliefs show the queen and the goddess together.

The construction of the High Dam at Aswan in the 1960s created a huge lake that would have drowned many Nubian monuments, including Abu Simbel. A big rescue mission was funded by UNESCO (United Nations Educational, Scientific and Cultural Organization). The temples were taken apart and put back together in a safe place beside the lake.

The Great Temple at Abu Simbel.

The Great Temple during reconstruction.

Rameses II offers **perfume** to Osiris in a painted scene from the temple at Abydos.

Abydos

Abydos is one of the most ancient and mysterious of Egyptian royal cities. It was inhabited from **Predynastic** times and may even have been the country's first capital. In **Early Dynastic** times Egypt's first kings were buried there in brick-lined pits marked by **stelae** carved with their names. Later Egyptians thought that one of these **tombs** contained the body of the god **Osiris**, and from the **Middle Kingdom** Abydos became the main centre of his worship.

Because Osiris was the lord of the underworld, people believed that being buried close to him at Abydos would guarantee them a good **afterlife**. Of course this was not always possible. Those who could not manage it sometimes tried to get the god's blessing by setting up stelae, or dummy tombs called cenotaphs, close to his temple. The pharaoh, who was believed to become Osiris when he died, sometimes built himself a memorial temple nearby. The most famous memorial temple at Abydos was built by the pharaoh Sety I.

Every year Abydos was the scene of a great **festival** that was meant to ensure the stability and prosperity of Egypt. The death and resurrection of Osiris was acted out in a series of plays including mock battles, which sometimes got a bit too realistic, resulting in accidents and even death. The festival attracted crowds of pilgrims from all over Egypt; all pious Egyptians hoped to visit Abydos at some time in their lives, and some even had paintings in their tombs showing their **mummies** being taken there after death.

Afterlife

The ancient Egyptians believed that every human being had spiritual elements that survived death. The most important spiritual elements were the *ka* and the *ba*. The *ka* was born with a person and was his or her life-force. It was shown as a person's double. After death, the *ka* seems to have needed a body to live in. This was one of the main reasons for mummifying bodies (see **Mummies**). If the mummy was lost or damaged, the *ka* could inhabit a statue instead. The *ka* also needed nourishment to survive. **Offering** spells in tombs promise eternal supplies of bread, beer and 'all good things on a which a god lives' for the *ka*.

The *ba* held the memory and personality of the dead person. It was usually shown as a bird with a human head and arms. The *ba* had the power to visit the world of the living in bird form. The **Greeks** misunderstood this and thought the Egyptians believed that the dead would be reincarnated as birds or animals. Soon after death the *ba* had to make a dangerous journey to the place where the spirits of the dead were judged. In early times the Egyptians believed that the dead joined the

A dead Egyptian meets gods and demons in the underworld and works in the fields of paradise.

stars high above the earth. Later the afterlife seems to take place below the earth. Everything in this 'underworld' was the reverse of normal, so people feared that they might be stuck upside-down and forced to eat their own excrement instead of food. Spells in the **Book of the Dead** promise to protect the *ba* from these bizarre fates.

The journey through the underworld was rather like an adventure game. The dead faced many demons and monsters, but they also met many magical helpers. The goal of this infernal game was to become an *akh*, a shining and powerful spirit. If the dead person passed through all the dangers of the underworld and was judged to have lived a good life, he or she would be turned into an *akh*. Those who failed these magical tests were destroyed.

Ancient Egyptian writings give many different views of what the afterlife would be like. One was that the blessed dead would 'repeat life' in a place called the 'Field of Reeds'. This was similar to Egypt, only better, and people would be reunited with their families there. It was said that an hour in the Field of Reeds was like a whole lifetime on earth. As an

*A person's **ba** was usually shown as a bird with a human head.*

akh the dead person might shine among the stars at the North Pole, which never seem to set, or serve in the court of **Osiris**, the king of the dead.

Another view was that the blessed dead would join the sun god **Ra** in the 'Boat of Millions' (see **Underworld Books**). All these ideas of the afterlife were thought to be equally true. The different spiritual elements of a person could be in several places at once.

Akhenaten

Akhenaten was ancient Egypt's most controversial ruler. His original name was Amenhotep and he was born in the 14th century BC, a younger son of King **Amenhotep III** and his chief wife Queen Tiy. When his older brother died, Akhenaten became heir to the throne. He became king in 1352 BC and may have ruled jointly with his father for several years. Akhenaten and the royal family started to worship a new god instead of Amun. This was Aten, the visible sun disc.

The young king's first major project was to build a great temple in **Thebes** to the god Aten. Akhenaten and his beautiful chief wife **Nefertiti** were shown on the walls of this temple, adoring the sun disc. Colossal statues showed the king with a long bony face and an almost female body. It has been suggested that Akhenaten had a rare disease that distorts the body, but these strange statues were probably just meant to make him look less human and more godlike.

By Year 5 of his reign the king had changed his name to Akhenaten ('Effective Spirit of the Aten'). He ordered a new capital, Akhetaten, to be built at a place now known as Tell el-**Amarna**. Other kings had founded cities and made their favourite gods the most important in Egypt, but Akhenaten went on to do something that no one had done before. He closed down most of the temples of the other gods. There was to be only one god, Aten, and Akhenaten was his representative on earth. All the temples at Akhetaten were dedicated to Aten. People had to worship images of Akhenaten and his family being blessed by the sun disc, even in their own homes.

The character of Akhenaten has fascinated people ever since his city was discovered. Some see him as a dreamy poet, others as a cruel tyrant. He was probably both. Akhenaten may be the author of two beautiful hymns to Aten and he took a close interest in the new style of art that was developed during his reign. He tried to force everyone to follow his ideas, but his new religion took away the Egyptians' freedom of choice and offered little hope of a happy **afterlife**. Thousands of people worked for temples, so closing them down caused hardship.

King Akhenaten with his wife **Nefertiti** *and three of their daughters. The god Aten is shown as a sun disc with rays ending in hands that hold out symbols of life to the royal family.*

Akhenaten reigned for sixteen years. A few years after his death the court moved back to Thebes and **Memphis** and the temples of the other gods were reopened. Mystery surrounds the fate of Akhenaten's body. It was probably deliberately destroyed. Akhenaten's name was left out of the official list of kings and no prayers were said for him in temples. If his reign had to be mentioned in legal documents he was referred to as 'The Great Criminal'. The ancient Egyptians wanted Akhenaten and his ideas to be forgotten.

Alexandria

Alexander the Great.

Roman tombs in Alexandria were decorated in a mixture of Egyptian and Roman styles.

The city of Alexandria was named after the brilliant **Greek** general Alexander the Great, who planned it as the capital of his empire. It lies on Egypt's northern coast, close to the western edge of the Nile Delta. The site was chosen by Alexander himself, but he did not live to see the city completed. In 323 BC, just nine years after he had conquered Egypt, he died in Babylon. His body was brought back to Alexandria to be buried, but the site of his tomb has never been found. All the same, the city flourished under his successors the **Ptolemies**, and later the **Romans**, becoming famous as a great centre of **trade** and learning. People called Alexandria the 'Queen of the Mediterranean', and the city was often represented in art as a beautiful woman with a ship on her head.

Alexandria was more like a Greek city than an Egyptian one. Its streets were laid out in a regular grid that divided the city into districts. There were two harbours, **temples** and **cemeteries**, baths and schools, shops and elegant villas, a museum and a library, a theatre, and a hippodrome for chariot racing. The dead were buried in elaborate underground catacombs. The lighthouse on Pharos Island at Alexandria was one of the Seven Wonders of the Ancient World, but it was destroyed in ancient times.

Painted pavement from a royal palace at Amarna.

Amarna

Tell el-Amarna is the modern name for the site of the ancient city of Akhetaten ('The Horizon of the Aten'). It was the capital city of the pharaoh **Akhenaten**, who worshipped the sun disc Aten.

Construction of the city was begun around 1350 BC and abandoned about twenty years later. Between 20,000 and 50,000 people lived there during this time. Many buildings, especially the tombs cut into the nearby cliffs, were never completed, but what remains of the city is quite well preserved. At the centre of the city were the official buildings, including the royal palace and the temple of the Aten, with housing and working areas on the outskirts. Wall carvings often show Akhenaten driving his chariot along the broad main highway.

One of the most interesting houses belonged to a sculptor named Dhutmose, who made a beautiful sculpture of the head of Akhenaten's wife **Nefertiti**, which is now in Berlin. This is a good example of the 'Amarna style' of art, which is usually very true to life. Amarna artists used flowing lines and vivid colours and loved to represent scenes from the natural world. In many of the houses and palaces of Akhetaten the walls and floors were painted with pictures of plants and wildlife.

Amenhotep III

Amenhotep III came to the throne as a child. In the second year of his reign he married a girl called Tiy, who was the daughter of an army officer. The bodies of Queen Tiy's parents are among the best preserved of all Egyptian **mummies**. Amenhotep III later married several foreign princesses and two of his own daughters, but Tiy was always his chief **queen**. When there was a royal marriage or something else important happened, Amenhotep III sent out the news inscribed on **scarabs**, which was rather like issuing commemorative stamps. In Year 2 of his reign he sent out a scarab recording that he had hunted down ninety-six wild bulls. A scarab of Year 10 claimed that he had killed a total of 102 lions 'with his own arrows'.

Amenhotep III was one of Egypt's greatest builders. He built or rebuilt many temples and filled them with sculptures. Two portraits of the king are among the largest statues ever made in Egypt (see **Colossi of Memnon**). In some temples he

*This **scarab** records how many lions Amenhotep III killed during hunts.*

*A painted **stela** shows Amenhotep III as he may have looked near the end of his life.*

was shown as a god being worshipped by himself. Statues of Amenhotep III show him as young and handsome. In reality he seems to have been overweight and plagued by dental problems. His poor health may have led the king to rule with his son, who later became **Akhenaten**.

Amenhotep is also known by the Greek version of his name, Amenophis.

Amulets

Amulets have been found everywhere that the ancient Egyptians lived, worked or buried their dead. People wore them to bring them luck and protect them from danger. There were hundreds of different types of amulet and each one was once the treasured possession of a particular person. The Egyptians thought that women and children needed amulets more than men did and some were made into attractive **jewellery**. People also believed that the neck and the belly-button were the most vulnerable parts of the body, so amuletic necklaces and belts were popular. Amulets could also be threaded on a leather thong and placed inside a cloth bag. Most Egyptian **clothes** had no pockets, so these amulet-bags were

*Amulets were often made of **gold** or gemstones. These amulets are all at least 4,000 years old.*

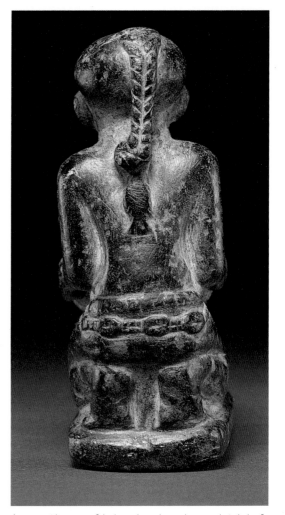

A young girl wears a fish-shaped amulet and an amuletic belt of cowrie shells.

usually hung round the neck. As soon as a baby was born, its nurse would make up a string of amulets for it.

Amulets were so important to the Egyptians in life that they thought the dead would need them too. They started to bury amulets with the dead over 7,000 years ago. These were usually just the lucky charms that people had owned when they were alive, but royalty and other rich and important people had specially-made amulets to protect them from the dangers they might face in the **afterlife**. By the 1st millennium BC most **mummies** were equipped with about 100 amulets, which were placed in the mummy wrapping to guard every part of the body. Spells had to be said over the amulets to make them work.

The shape, colour and material of an amulet were important. Many were in the form of **gods** or their **sacred animals** because the wearers hoped that the power of the god would help and protect them. The **scarab** beetle and the **Eye of Horus** were the most popular amulets. Red amulets were supposed to be good at warding off danger but blue-green was the favourite colour because it stood for life, new growth and good health. **Gold** doesn't tarnish, so people believed that gold amulets kept their power for ever.

The Egyptians thought that writing had its own **magic** power. Some people protected themselves by wearing the **name** of a god or a king inscribed on a scarab or written on scraps of linen or **papyrus**. Some children wore a special kind of amulet known as an **oracle** papyrus. In return for gifts a temple would issue a certificate promising the child divine protection against all sorts of dangers, including getting worms, catching the plague, being haunted by angry ghosts or demons, drowning in the river and being buried by a collapsing house. The certificate was rolled up small and put in a leather or metal case which the child wore for life.

Amun

Amun was the most mysterious of the Egyptian gods. His name can also be spelled Amon or Amen and probably meant 'The Hidden One'. Amun is first mentioned along with the goddess Amunet, though they are not husband and wife, but male and female forms of the same deity. Amun and Amunet were part of the Ogdoad of **Hermopolis**, eight deities who ruled the endless dark waters of chaos before the world was made (see **Creation myths**). Amun came to symbolize the hidden power of life.

At **Thebes**, Amun was said to be the husband of the goddess Mut and the

father of the moon god Khons. He was usually shown as a man wearing a false beard and a cap with two tall feathers. His skin was sometimes painted sky blue. Amun's **sacred animals** were the goose and the short-horned ram and he himself sometimes took the form of a goose, a ram, or a snake with a ram's head. He could be linked with other deities too. As Amun-**Min** he was the power of sex and as Amun-**Ra** he was the creator of all life.

By the **New Kingdom** Amun was known as the king of the gods. Some rulers of Egypt claimed to be children of Amun. Others believed that he fought by their side and helped them gain victory in battle. These grateful kings gave land and treasure to Amun in return and his temple at **Karnak** became the largest and richest in all Egypt.

In spite of being such an important god, Amun was 'the one who comes at the voice of the poor', who listened to ordinary people's prayers and forgave their sins. He became a popular god outside Egypt too, and was worshipped by the Libyans (see **Egypt's neighbours**) and by the peoples of **Nubia,** where he was the god of the holy mountain at Gebel Barkal. The kings of this region called themselves 'Sons of Amun' and his cult lived on in Nubia even after it had died out in Egypt.

A gold and silver figure of Amun.

From a prayer to Amun, written around the 12th century BC:
My Lord is my defender, I know his strength,
He helps with a strong arm and a compassionate look.
He alone is the powerful one.
Amun knows how to be kind, and hears anyone who cries out to him.
Amun, King of the Gods, mighty bull, glorious in his power.

Animals

Animals played a central role in Egyptian life from the earliest times. The first Egyptians were hunters who depended on wild game for survival, and throughout Egyptian history **hunting** was enjoyed by rich and poor alike. The plentiful lake and river **fish** were another source of food available to everyone. By the **Old Kingdom** many animal species had been domesticated. Cattle provided meat, milk and leather, and sheep and goats gave wool as well as meat.

Birds were an important source of eggs, meat and feathers: ducks, geese and pigeons were hunted in the wild and also raised in large poultry yards attached to temples and country estates, though chickens did not become common until **Graeco-Roman** times. Bees provided honey for sweetening food.

The Egyptians also used animals such as oxen and donkeys as beasts of burden. Horses, which were introduced by the Hyksos (see **Egypt's neighbours**) after the **Middle Kingdom**, were used to pull chariots (see **Travel**) and were also crossed with donkeys to produce strong working mules. People admired other animals for their grace, beauty or entertainment value: favourite pets included **cats**, **dogs**, monkeys and gazelles, and exotic animals were imported as curiosities. The importance of animals to the Egyptians can be seen from the large number of **gods and goddesses** with animal features, and the many cults devoted to **sacred animals**.

Cats were sacred to the goddess Bastet.

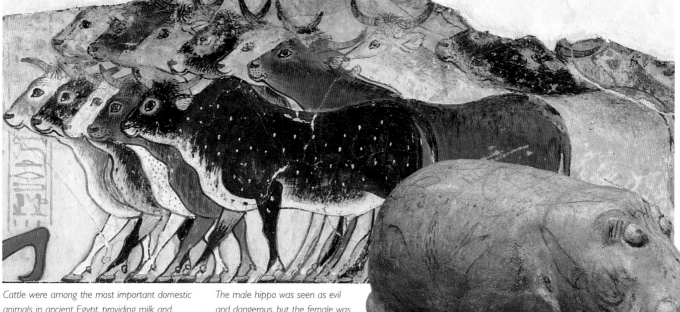

Cattle were among the most important domestic animals in ancient Egypt, providing milk and dairy foods, meat, leather and dung for fuel. Farmers also used oxen as working animals and gave their favourites names like 'Good-Flood-Comes'!

The male hippo was seen as evil and dangerous, but the female was worshipped as the goddess of childbearing. Faience hippos like this one were often offered to the goddess Hathor.

Ankh

A hieroglyphic sign for the word 'life', which was also used as an amulet.

Anubis

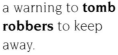

Anubis was the canine god of **cemeteries** and he was the first god to be shown in non-royal tombs. He was portrayed as a black jackal-like creature or as a man with the head of a jackal. His most famous **temple** was at a town which the **Greeks** called Cynopolis ('City of the Dogs'). Scavenging jackals and wild dogs often disturbed shallow desert graves and the ancient Egyptians tried to get these creatures on their side by honouring Anubis. The image of the jackal was also a warning to **tomb robbers** to keep away.

In early times Anubis was the chief god of the dead but this role was gradually taken over by **Osiris**. Some versions of the Osiris story made Anubis his son. The Egyptians believed that Anubis invented mummification to preserve the body of Osiris (see **Mummies**). Embalmers sometimes wore Anubis masks and they were called 'Anubis-men'. They were outcasts because of their profession.

Every tomb in the **Valley of the Kings** was sealed with an image of a jackal to show that Anubis was guarding

*This jackal mask would have been worn by a **priest** or an embalmer playing the role of Anubis. There are eye-holes under the chin.*

the royal dead. A famous statue of Anubis as a jackal was found in **Tutankhamun**'s tomb.

Apis bull

The Apis bull was like a national mascot for ancient Egypt. For over 3,000 years a special bull was picked to live in the temple of **Ptah** at **Memphis**. This bull was honoured as the soul of the god Ptah when he was alive and as a form of the god **Osiris** after he died. An Apis bull had to be mainly black, with a white patch on the brow and a special **scarab**-shaped mark on its tongue. **Priests** searched all over Egypt to find the right calf, which was then crowned as if it was a king and taken to live in a special enclosure that was like a miniature palace.

The bull's stall had two doors, one lucky and one unlucky, and the priests claimed that they could tell the future of Egypt by watching which door the Apis bull used. On certain days the public were allowed to visit the enclosure. Many people believed that if the Apis bull took some food from their hand they would have good luck. When an Apis bull died. it was mummified and given a state funeral (see **Mummies**).

Apis bulls were buried in tombs on the edge of the desert.

Apophis

The Great Tom-Cat cuts off the head of the **snake** Apophis.

The ancient Egyptians felt that their world was always in danger of slipping back into chaos and considered Apophis (Apep) to be the most dangerous of the chaos monsters. One myth says that he was born from the saliva of the goddess **Neith**. Apophis was usually shown as a huge snake. Every night he attacked the boat of the sun (see **Underworld Books**) and had to be beaten back by the strongest of the gods. One of these gods was the Great Tom-Cat, who cut off his head. Apophis could be killed but he always came back to life again.

On temple walls the king was occasionally shown playing a game that looks rather like baseball. The ball which he had to hit was called 'The Eye of Apophis' and the game was a symbol of the victory of order over chaos. Priests acted out the unending war against chaos by drawing pictures of Apophis on **papyrus**. The pictures were then cursed, stabbed and burned, and the ashes were left to dissolve in a bucket of urine.

Architecture

The first buildings in Egypt were made from the natural materials that people found around them – Nile mud, reeds and the trunks and fronds of palm trees. Tents and reed shelters were cool to live in and quick to put up, while mud was ideal for more permanent buildings. Villagers in the Egyptian countryside still use these materials to build their homes, which look very similar to ancient Egyptian houses.

Mud bricks are made from Nile mud mixed with water and chopped straw, then shaped in a mould and left to dry in the hot sun. Mud-brick buildings had to be strong to survive the Nile flood, so the walls were made thicker at the bottom and sloped inwards for stability. Their flat roofs were made of palm logs supported by wooden columns. Doors and windows were small to keep the inside cool.

Mud-brick houses in the Egyptian countryside have hardly changed since ancient times.

Types of Egyptian columns:
A   Palm
B   Lotus
C   Papyrus bundle
C   Open papyrus
E   Closed papyrus

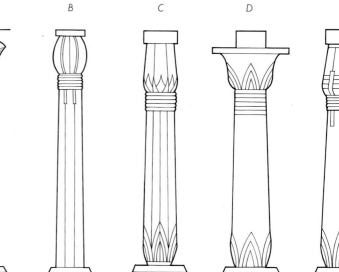

This **Middle Kingdom** rock-cut tomb at **Beni Hasan** belonged to a local governor called Khmunhotep.

These **Old Kingdom** shrines at Saqqara were built with **stone** blocks but they imitate shelters made from reeds and tree trunks.

From the beginning of the **Old Kingdom** architects began to use **stone** for royal monuments and religious buildings, such as **pyramids**, **temples** and **tombs**. They knew that stone would last longer than mud bricks.

There were two types of stone architecture. Masonry buildings were constructed from stone blocks. Rock-cut tombs and temples were carved out of cliffs and hillsides (see **Building**). Although stone is quite different from wood or mud-brick, the architects often copied features of traditional wooden and brick buildings into stone.

Temples usually have sloping walls, with rounded corners that look rather like tent poles; some are even carved with designs representing the ropes that held the original structure together. The columns that hold up the roof often imitate wooden posts or bundles of reeds and are set close together, as they would be in a building roofed with palm logs. This was probably because the Egyptians believed it was important for religious buildings to conform to ancient conventions.

Army

The Egyptian army was more of a general task force than a strictly military organization. It provided men for jobs like trading expeditions or moving **obelisks** as well as for fighting and guard duties. For most of Egyptian history the army was made up of a small core of professional soldiers, with extra troops being drafted when they were needed. Foreign mercenaries – often from **Nubia** or Libya (see **Egypt's neighbours**) – played an increasingly important role from the **Middle Kingdom** onwards. By the **New Kingdom** the land army had been organized into foot and chariot divisions and there was a navy as well.

Soldiers and sailors were armed with bows or spears, swords or daggers. Armour was rare and most men fought in a simple loincloth. Their only protection was a shield made of wood covered in leather. Soldiers were given food rations and were paid according to their performance in battle. They received **gold**, land and **slaves** depending on how

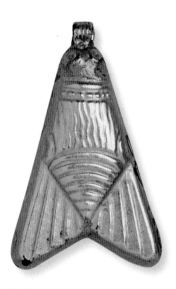

Gold flies were the Egyptian equivalent of military medals. Brave soldiers were compared to flies – however often they are swatted away, they come back again!

Soldiers of Queen **Hatshepsut**'s *army on a trading expedition. The goods they have come to trade are piled up in front of them.*

Description of a soldier's life:

Let me tell you how it is for the soldier ...
Here for you is his trip to Syria, his march over the hills! His bread and water are across his shoulder like a donkey's load ...
He only gets to drink water every three days, and then it is polluted and salty. His body is racked with diarrhoea.
The enemy come – they pin him in with arrows, all hope of life seems far from him ...
He succeeds in getting back to Egypt, but he's like a worm-eaten stick – ill, weak, brought in on a donkey's back. His clothes are stolen, and his attendant runs away ... give up the idea that the soldier is better off than the scribe!

many of the enemy they had managed to kill or capture. They sometimes had to cut off their victims' hands to prove how many they had killed. Joining the army was one way a poor man could make his fortune and many boys were tempted by the prospect of riches and foreign travel. In an attempt to put them off engaging in **warfare**, teachers made their pupils copy out texts describing the hardships and dangers of army life!

Art

Egyptian art was associated with **magic** from the earliest times. Prehistoric hunters made rock drawings of animals as a way of gaining power over them. It was probably for the same reason that the first **kings** had carvings made showing them as victorious conquerors, grabbing a kneeling enemy by the hair and threatening him with a mace, or club. Amazingly, over 3,000 years later the **Ptolemies** were still being represented in the same way in scenes carved on the front of **temples**.

Egyptian artists were very traditional and tended to copy the work of previous generations, probably because they thought there was some special power in

Human figures had to be drawn to a complicated set of proportions. The more important people were, the bigger they were shown.

the ancient ways of showing things. This power was important to them because most art had some magical purpose. Paintings, carvings and models in tombs were there to provide for the needs of the dead in the next life. Reliefs were carved on temple walls to ensure that the **gods** would always overcome evil.

Egyptians thought that pictures had power, so they represented everything very carefully. Dangerous things were changed to make them harmless. Scorpions were often shown without their legs or stingers. Many of the king's belongings, such as his walking stick and footstool, were decorated with images of Egypt's foes, tied up and helpless.

Artists had to show things as clearly as possible or their work could not perform its **magic**. This was quite easy in sculpture, but it was more complicated in paintings and wall carvings. So artists arranged the things they wanted to show into horizontal bands called 'registers' to help make things clear. These bands look rather like comic strips, although there is no background to tell us where things are happening, and the scenes do not always follow each other in the right order. Solid objects (like people and furniture) were drawn as they appeared from the side, and flat objects (like loaves of bread and necklaces) as they appeared from above. When artists wanted to show that a box had things inside it, they showed the contents on top of the box or made the sides transparent.

People were shown with their head, arms, hands, hips, legs and feet seen from the side, and their eyes, chest and shoulders seen from the front. The proportions of the figure were strictly controlled: the head, for example, was equal to one-ninth of the total height. The larger a person was shown, the more important he or she was: gods and kings were bigger than mortals, the nobility bigger than their **servants**, husbands bigger than their wives, and parents bigger than their **children**. In **tombs**, people were shown in the way they wanted to be remembered. Even people who lived to an old age were portrayed as young, healthy and good-looking! (See also **Painting and drawing** and **Sculpture**.)

Ivory label showing the 1st-Dynasty king Den threatening a foreign enemy.

Nearly 3,000 years later, Ptolemy XIII was shown in the same way on the front of Edfu temple.

*Wall painting of a **garden** pond. Egyptian artists drew solid objects as they appeared from the side and flat objects as if seen from above.*

Aswan

The modern city of Aswan in southern Egypt is built around the first Nile cataract, where huge islands of granite block the river, making it impossible for boats to pass. In ancient times this natural barrier formed Egypt's southern border and the town grew up around the garrison stationed there to protect it. Aswan's granite quarries became an important source of **stone** for buildings, royal statues and sarcophagi. Visitors still come to the quarries to marvel at a huge unfinished **obelisk** lying in the rock.

The ancient Egyptian name for Aswan was Abu, which means 'elephant', and the **Greeks** called its biggest island Elephantine. Perhaps it got this name because the big grey rocks of the cataract look a bit like elephants bathing in the water, or perhaps it was because the town was an important trading centre for ivory and other exotic African products such as gold, incense and wild **animals**. The name Aswan probably comes from an ancient Egyptian word, *swenet*, meaning 'market'.

Aswan was also important to the ancient Egyptians as the mythological source of the River Nile, which they thought flowed from a cave under the cataract. Many temples were built to please the Nile god **Khnum** so that he would deliver the annual flood on which Egypt's farmers depended to grow their crops. As the waters rose each year, priests measured the height of the flood using a huge **Nilometer** on Elephantine Island.

Atum

The creator god Atum was head of the family of nine gods known as the Ennead of **Heliopolis**. He was also linked with the creative power of the sun and was worshipped as Atum-**Ra**, the setting sun. (See also **Creation myths** and **Underworld Books**.)

The city of Aswan.

Bastet

Bastet (or Pasht) was a feline goddess. She was one of the fierce goddesses who protected Egyptian **kings**. At first she was shown as a woman with the head of a lioness, though she was later given the more playful and affectionate qualities of a pet **cat**. Bastet came to be shown as a cat or as a woman with the head of a cat and was often contrasted with **Sekhmet**, the terrifying lioness goddess. One ancient Egyptian writer complained that women are like Bastet when they get their own way and like Sekhmet when they don't.

During the New Year holiday, people gave each other **amulets** of Bastet as presents to bring good luck. Those who wanted many children prayed to the goddess and bought a figurine of her with a litter of kittens. 'She whom Bastet gave' and 'Son of Bastet' were common Egyptian **names**. Bastet's chief **temple** was in the Delta, at a place the Egyptians called Per-Bastet (the house of Bastet) and the **Greeks** called Bubastis. The Greek writer Herodotus, who visited Egypt in the 5th century BC, saw a festival of the cat goddess. Thousands of pilgrims came by boat to Bubastis, where they spent several days making music, dancing and getting drunk. Lion-hunting was forbidden during this festival.

Hundreds of sacred cats lived in and around Bastet's temples and when they died they were mummified and buried in tunnels. Thousands of these cat **mummies** were shipped to Europe in the 19th century and ground up to be used as fertilizer.

A bronze figure of Bastet with four kittens.

B

Baboons helping to pick figs. Painting from the tomb of Khnumhotep at Beni Hasan.

Beni Hasan

The **cemetery** at Beni Hasan in Middle Egypt is set high up in the cliffs of the Nile's east bank. It is famous for the rock-cut **tombs** excavated there for **Middle Kingdom** noblemen. The walls of the tomb chapels are covered with colourful paintings of everyday life 4,000 years ago.

Bes

The dwarf god Bes dancing and playing a tambourine to scare away evil spirits.

The god Bes was part lion, part dwarf, and 'as ugly as an old monkey'. There was also a female form of Bes, who was known as Beset. These lion-dwarfs appear on **magic** wands with other monstrous creatures. They look terrifying, but the Egyptians called them 'the protectors'.

Bes pulled faces, stuck his tongue out, stamped his feet, and played noisy instruments such as the tambourine to scare off evil spirits. He banished anger and sadness with his music and **dances**.

Figures of Bes were often carved on bedroom **furniture**. The aim was to protect the sleeper from nightmares and from real dangers such as snakes, scorpions and biting insects. The ugly face of Bes also appears on many **cosmetic** pots and mirrors. Couples who wanted children spent the night in special rooms painted with images of Bes and pregnant women wore Bes **amulets** to help them give birth safely.

In **Roman** times magicians used spells to make them **dream** about Bes so that they could ask him questions. He was also consulted as an **oracle** in one of the temples at **Abydos**. When Christianity became the main religion of Egypt, helpful Bes was seen as a devil. A Coptic (see **Copts**) story tells of a brave monk who drove the hideous Bes demon out of Abydos. The Christians couldn't quite erase the memory of Bes, however. An ugly dwarf was said to haunt the ruined temple of **Karnak** in the 19th century.

Birds

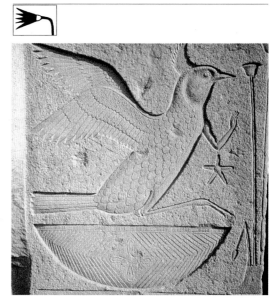

A lapwing carved on a temple column.

Egypt has always had a huge variety of bird life because it is on the main bird migration routes between Europe and Africa. Over seventy species have been identified in ancient Egyptian **art**. Birds were an important source of food from the earliest times (see **Hunting** and **Animals**) but they also had a symbolic meaning in art. Scenes of the king trapping wild birds and presenting them to the gods represented his victory over the forces of evil. The lapwing, often

Geese were kept for their meat, eggs and feathers.

Not all birds were useful or popular. Farmers had trouble with birds eating their crops. This New Kingdom text describes the Egyptian goose: *It spends the summer destroying the dates, and the winter destroying the wheat. It spends its free time following the farmers, and does not allow the seed to be thrown to the ground before it has got wind of it!*

Light rafts made from papyrus reeds were useful for hunting and fishing.

shown with human hands, symbolized the ordinary people of Egypt, while the goddess **Maat** was sometimes represented by the ostrich feather she wore on her head. The birds associated with certain **gods and goddesses** were sometimes worshipped. When they died, they were mummified and buried in special cemeteries (see **Sacred animals**).

Birds were often associated with the spirit world. The soul of a dead person, the *ba*, was represented as a human-headed bird, while the word *akh*, which described a person's form in the next world, was written with an ibis symbol. Other mythological birds included the Benu bird, or phoenix, which appears in scenes of the **afterlife**.

Boats

Because life in ancient Egypt centred around the River Nile, boats were very important. One of the first things the early Egyptians learned to do was to build rafts and skiffs from bundles of **papyrus** reeds tied together. These simple boats made it possible for people to cross the river, go fishing, hunt birds in the marshes, and travel to other villages. Water travel was very easy because the Nile flows from south to north and the wind in Egypt usually blows from north to south. So, to go north the Egyptian boatmen rowed with the current; to go south they put up a sail and let the wind carry them along.

Wooden model from a tomb, showing a mummy being transported by boat.

Ankhwa was a supervisor of boat builders during the Old Kingdom. He carries an adze (a long-handled tool used to shape boat timbers) as a sign of his office.

Boats were so necessary for getting around that they became firmly linked to the idea of **travel** – the words for travelling in different directions were written with signs showing a boat with its sail down (going north) or up (going south). The Nile teemed with activity. Almost every town had its riverside quay, while **temples** and palaces had their own private harbours, which were connected to the river by canals. Special types of boats were developed for travelling, **hunting**, fighting, **fishing** and transporting goods and **animals**. At **Memphis** the royal dockyards built fleets of warships for the navy. Ships were given names like 'Beloved of Amun'.

Although these boats varied in shape and size according to their purpose, their basic design remained much the same from the **Middle Kingdom** until **Graeco-Roman** times. They were broad and shallow with a high prow (front) and stern (back), and there was usually a cabin on the deck. At the stern was a large steering oar, sometimes with a shelter to protect the steersman from the hot sun. In the centre of the deck a tall mast held a large, oblong **linen** sail. Both sail and mast could be lowered when not in use. Timber was scarce, so boats were made up of many small pieces of wood held together by ropes or wooden pegs. Once the boat was in the water the timbers swelled up, sealing the cracks and stopping the boat from leaking.

Boats also played an important part in religion. The underworld was believed to be full of rivers and canals, like Egypt itself. **Mummies** were transported to their tombs on boat-shaped sleds, and paintings and models of boats were put into tombs to help the dead travel about in the next life. Even the **gods and goddesses** travelled in boats. The Egyptians thought that the sun god crossed the sky in one ship during the day and sailed through the underworld in another one at night. Paintings in royal tombs often show the dead king travelling in the boat of the sun (see **Underworld Books**). In the **Old Kingdom** full-sized ships were buried in pits alongside royal pyramids, perhaps to help their owners to journey through the underworld. During religious **festivals**,

statues of gods and goddesses were carried in boat-shaped shrines. At large temples, the most important gods and goddesses even had their own river barges to transport their images. On special occasions the king would appear before his people in his magnificent ship of state which, like the gods' barges, was elaborately carved and covered with **gold**. Wall carvings and paintings show these spectacular vessels being hauled down the Nile by excited crowds on the riverbanks, while musicians and dancers add to the happy atmosphere.

Book of the Dead

The 'Book of the Dead' is the modern name for a collection of spells which the ancient Egyptians called 'The Spells for Going Out by Day'. This collection was first used around 1600 BC, but some of the spells are much older than this. There are at least 190 chapters in the Book of the Dead but no single copy contains them all because people used to choose the chapters they wanted. The spells were usually written in **hieroglyphs** on rolls of **papyrus**. Copies made for rich and important people had beautiful illustrations. Full versions of the Book of

the Dead can be up to 30 m (90 ft) long.

Some of the chapters were spells that priests recited during a person's mummification (see **Mummies**) and **funeral**. The rest were a guide to survival in the **afterlife**. The Book of the Dead promises to reveal the secrets of the underworld. The illustrations show the spirit of the dead man or woman facing all kinds of dangers, from demons who caught the dead in fishing nets to hungry crocodiles. Knowing the **names** of the demons and monsters in the underworld could be enough to control them. In some spells the dead person takes on the powers of various gods in order to battle against demons and win a place in heaven.

The most famous section of the Book of the Dead is Chapter 125, which describes how a person's soul will be judged in the afterlife. The dead person had to be able to plead innocent to a long list of sins. This was known as the 'Negative Confession'. Then the person's heart would be placed on a pair of scales and weighed against the feather of **Maat** (Truth). Those who survived the judgement became blessed spirits. Then they could use spells from the Book of the Dead to turn themselves into birds and visit the world of the living by day.

*Part of Chapter 125 in a beautifully illustrated copy of the Book of the Dead. The owner of this copy is shown being tried in the court of **Osiris**, the king of the underworld.*

Part of an ancient mud-brick builders' ramp at Karnak temple. Some of the columns in the corner of the courtyard were never finished.

Building

Buildings in ancient Egypt were usually made of mud-brick or **stone**. Mud-brick was used for most everyday buildings, such as houses, offices, workshops, stores and even royal palaces. Stone was mostly used for religious buildings like **tombs** and **temples**, which were intended to last forever. Mud-brick was a very practical material. It was a good insulator so it helped keep the inside of the buildings cool in hot weather. Above all, it was easy to build with. The Egyptians were expert bricklayers, using bricks to build all kinds of structures from vaulted storerooms to huge forts and massive city walls.

The simplest type of stone buildings were the rock-cut monuments, which were carved out of the cliffs alongside the Nile Valley using methods learned from stone quarrying. The men worked in two teams, one on the left and one on the right. Each part of the team had a special job. The first to start work were the excavators, who cut out the rough shape of the monument. They were followed by the masons, who smoothed the walls and shaped the columns that supported the roof. Next were the sculptors, who shaped the statues and did the carvings on the walls. Last of all came the plasterers and painters, who added the final touches. Among Egypt's most famous rock-cut monuments are the royal tombs in the **Valley of the Kings** and the great temples at **Abu Simbel**.

Masonry monuments – most temples and some types of tomb – were built using stone blocks, which was more difficult. First the stone had to be quarried and brought to the site. This was hard work, so where possible the builders used local stone (limestone in the north of Egypt and sandstone in the south). The quarried blocks were brought to the building site by river, then taken to where they were needed on sleds or rollers.

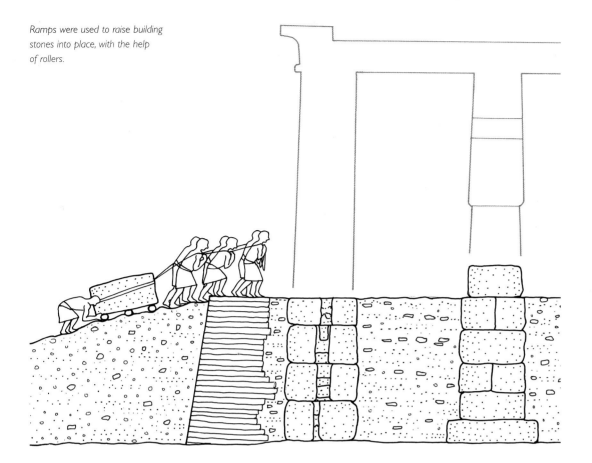

Ramps were used to raise building stones into place, with the help of rollers.

Before building work started the sides of the blocks were rubbed with sand until they were perfectly straight and smooth. They could then be fitted together without needing mortar to hold them in place.

Walls were built into a foundation trench filled with sand. When the first layer of stones had been laid, workers built a brick ramp so that they could drag the blocks for the next layer up to where they were needed. The ramp was raised as each layer was completed until the builders reached the top. Then they began to take the ramp apart, smoothing off the outside of the wall on the way down. Columns could also be built in the same way, although they were sometimes made from a single piece of hard stone, such as granite. Roofs were usually made of flat slabs of stone. Sometimes a part of the roof was raised to make a space for window grilles to let in light and air; otherwise, windows were just small slits cut high up in the walls.

Private building work was usually carried out by the estate-owner's own workers or by other workmen employed by him, but royal building projects were supervised by the king's officials. **Scribes** were trained to work out the number of men and the amounts of time and materials needed for a specific project. Royal architects needed to be experts in understanding the structure of buildings, but sometimes they made mistakes and buildings fell down in earthquakes, or even collapsed under their own weight!

Major royal building works were often carried out during the flood season, when large numbers of farmworkers had nothing to do. Royal officials went round the countryside enlisting strong men to work as unskilled labourers, moving the great blocks of stone around. The skilled workers, such as masons and sculptors, were state employees, paid in goods such as **food**, cloth and oil (see **Deir el-Medina**). Sometimes, when their supplies were late in coming, they went on strike until they got them!

During the reign of Rameses III, supplies to the royal builders were often interrupted. Finally the workmen had had enough and went on strike. They occupied the courtyard of the local temple where supplies were kept and sent this message to the official in charge: *It is because of hunger and because of thirst that we come here. There is no clothing, no ointment, no fish, no vegetables. Send to Pharaoh our good lord about it, and send to the vizier our superior, so that provision may be made for us.*

Canopic jars

When people died in ancient Egypt their bodies were preserved by mummification (see **Mummies**). To help prevent a body decaying, the internal organs were removed and placed inside special containers known as canopic jars. To keep the organs safe, the jars were often sealed with stoppers shaped like the heads of four gods known as the Sons of **Horus**. Hapy, with an ape's head, looked after the lungs. Imsety, with a man's head, looked after the liver. Qebehsenuef, with a hawk's head, looked after the

Canopic jars.

intestines. And Duamutef, with a jackal's head, looked after the stomach.

Canopic jars get their name from the town of Canopus in the Nile Delta, where the people used to worship **Osiris** in the shape of a jar with a human head on top. Because the jars used in mummification looked similar, early **Egyptologists** called them 'canopic' jars.

Cartonnage

Cartonnage is a strong, light material made from layers of **linen** or **papyrus** strengthened with plaster. It is rather like papier mâché and is easy to mould into shape. Cartonnage could be gilded or painted in bright colours and was often used to make masks and cases for mummies.

Cartonnage mummy mask of a **Middle Kingdom** princess.

Cartouche

'Cartouche' is the modern word for the oval used to encircle the **names** of Egyptian **kings** and **queens**. Today visitors to Egypt often have their names written in **hieroglyphs** inside a cartouche, but in ancient times it was a crime for anyone but royalty to do this. Most Egyptian kings had many names. The two

The names of kings and queens were written inside oval cartouches.

most important ones, the throne name and the personal name, were given a cartouche to make them stand out. Gods' names were sometimes written within cartouches too.

Elaborately carved or painted versions show that the cartouche was meant to represent a coiled rope, tied up at one end. It is a based on a hieroglyph called the *shen* sign, which stands for 'everything that the sun encircles'. By placing their names inside cartouches Egyptian kings were claiming to be rulers of the world. A cartouche also put them under the protection of the sun god. That is why some kings were buried in cartouche-shaped coffins and ordinary people wore cartouche-shaped **amulets**.

The term 'cartouche' comes from a French word for an oval gun cartridge and was first used by the scholars who accompanied the Emperor Napoleon when he invaded Egypt in 1798. Several people who tried to decipher the hieroglyphic script realized that the cartouches held royal names. The French genius Jean-François Champollion finally deciphered the cartouches of **Ptolemy** and **Cleopatra** (see **Rosetta Stone**).

Cats

Cats were highly valued in ancient Egypt, both as pets and as working **animals** who kept the granaries free of mice. Some cats were even trained to help out on **hunting** trips by bringing back birds which their masters had stunned with throwing-sticks. A pet cat was treated like a member of the family. Tomb paintings often show cats and kittens sitting underneath their owners' chairs, sometimes with a dish of food nearby. Some cats wore collars, while others had their ears pierced and fitted with **gold** or silver earrings. When pets died, the family who had owned them went into mourning. Favourite cats were mummified after death, and some even had their own sarcophagi (see **Coffins**).

Cats were also considered to be **sacred animals** because of their association with gods and goddesses such as **Bastet**. Thousands of mummified cats were buried close to Bastet's temple at Bubastis, and visiting pilgrims often made offerings of cat statues.

Cats were treated with great respect. This beautiful cast-bronze cat wears silver amulets and gold ear- and nose-rings, just as pampered cats did in real life.

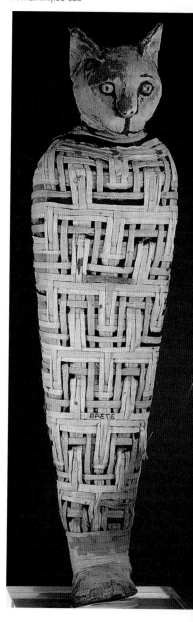

A mummified cat.

Royal cemeteries in Egypt were built as 'cities of the dead'. These two pictures show cemeteries at Giza (above) and Thebes (below).

Cemeteries

The Greek word 'necropolis', which means 'city of the dead', is often used to describe an Egyptian cemetery. The realm of the dead was thought to be in the 'Beautiful West' because that was where the sun set, so Egyptians preferred their cemeteries to be on the west bank of the River Nile. Because agricultural land was precious, people were buried on the edge of the desert or on sand-hills in the marshy Delta. Every town and city had at least one cemetery. Many cemetery sites were chosen because they had cliffs suitable for rock-cut **tombs**, or **stone** for **pyramids** or **mastaba** tombs.

Until the 16th century BC important people were often buried close to the tombs of the **kings** they had served. There were major royal cemeteries at **Abydos**, el-Lisht, **Giza** and **Saqqara**. These last two sites were part of the great cemetery for **Memphis**, which stretched for over 30 km (19 miles). Royal cemeteries were carefully planned. They were laid out like towns with tombs instead of houses and sometimes old tombs had to be knocked down or altered to make way for new roads through the cemetery. Government officials patrolled the cemeteries to guard against **tomb robbers**. In theory only the king could grant someone the right to build in a royal cemetery, so having a large tomb close to a royal burial place was just as important as living at a good address in life.

Royal burial customs changed in the **New Kingdom**. For around 500 years kings were buried in underground tombs in the **Valley of the Kings** at **Thebes**. Only a few favoured courtiers were given tombs in the royal valley. The rest had to build tombs elsewhere in western Thebes, or in the old royal cemeteries of Memphis. After the New Kingdom, kings and **queens** were usually buried in the grounds of **temples**, such as the temple of the god **Amun** at Tanis.

People didn't just go to cemeteries for **funerals**. Regular visits were made to family tombs and drinking parties were held there to bring the living and the dead together. Images of **gods and goddesses** were carried through cemeteries during some religious **festivals**. Pilgrims came to pray in or near the special cemeteries for **sacred animals**. These were usually a maze of tunnels with thousands of animals buried in pots or boxes in niches in the walls. People also visited cemeteries to admire the **art** in the open areas of tombs. The cemeteries of Memphis have been called 'the world's biggest art gallery'.

Children

Children were central to **family** life in ancient Egypt. People believed strongly in the **afterlife** so they wanted children to make sure their **funeral** rites would be performed properly. If people could not have children they sometimes adopted orphans. Sadly, children themselves often died young because of accident or disease, even though their parents tried to protect them with **magic** and **amulets**. These early deaths made the children who survived even more precious.

The closeness between parents and children is seen most clearly in **tombs**, where children are usually shown making offerings to their dead parents. Younger children are generally shown with their heads shaved, apart from a single lock of **hair** on the side of the head. Otherwise there were few differences in appearance between adults and children. Although the youngest children ran about naked, older children dressed like their parents

and painted their eyes in the same way (see **Cosmetics**).

In **art** children were often shown with a finger pointing to their lips, showing that they still depended on their parents for food. In real life, though, they often had to work from an early age. Tomb paintings show farmworkers' children helping with the harvest and minding **animals**, while the sons of craftsmen learned the family trade by watching their fathers at work, helping them out by doing small chores and running errands. In general, only the sons of the wealthy were educated (see **Education**). Girls usually stayed at home to help their mothers with housework, but some also worked as **servants** in wealthy homes, where they often got the chance to learn crafts such as weaving. Children whose parents could not afford to look after them were sometimes given to a temple or sold as **slaves**. They had to work for their owners for the rest of their lives.

When there was no work to do, children amused themselves with a variety of **sports** such as leapfrog, ball games and tug-of-war. Some were lucky enough to have simple **toys** like balls and tops to play with.

*Queen **Hatshepsut**'s daughter Neferura with her tutor Senenmut. The little princess wears a single lock of hair and points to her mouth to show she is still a child.*

Cleopatra VII

The name Cleopatra ('famous in her father') was given to many princesses among the **Ptolemies**, a **Greek** family who ruled Egypt for 300 years. Several of these princesses married close relatives and became queens of Egypt or Syria. By the 1st century BC the Ptolemies were in danger of losing their independence to the growing power of Rome (see **Romans**). Queen Cleopatra VII was the favourite daughter of Ptolemy XII. Although not particularly beautiful, she was clever, charming and sexy. Cleopatra and her half-brother Ptolemy XIII became rulers of Egypt in 51 BC. Ptolemy XIII soon drove his sister out of the capital, but she found a protector in the great Roman general, Julius Caesar. Ptolemy XIII was killed after a civil war and Caesar made Cleopatra queen of Egypt, although she had to share the throne with her youngest half-brother.

After Julius Caesar had left Egypt for Rome, Cleopatra gave birth to a son, whom she called Caesarion, claiming that he was Caesar's child. Cleopatra was visiting Rome when Caesar was murdered by his political enemies, but she tried not to take sides in the civil war that followed. When her half-brother died, Cleopatra made Caesarion her co-ruler in Egypt, and her native Egyptian subjects thought of her as being like another single mother, the great goddess **Isis**.

By this time, Caesar's great-nephew Octavian (Augustus) and the Roman general Mark Antony had become joint rulers of Rome. In 41 BC Cleopatra was summoned to Tarsus by Mark Antony. They began a long love affair, even though Antony soon had to marry Octavian's sister for political reasons.

Cleopatra had three children by Mark Antony and used her wealth to pay for his armies. In return for her support Antony made **Alexandria** the capital of a new empire to be ruled by Cleopatra and her children, but this led to a war with Rome. After months of fighting, Antony and Cleopatra's fleet was defeated at the Battle of Actium. When Octavian's army was close to Alexandria, Antony killed himself. Cleopatra was captured, and she poisoned herself soon afterwards. Octavian then had Caesarion murdered and made Egypt part of the Roman Empire (see **Graeco-Roman Period**).

Cleopatra was remembered as a great queen who had fought to keep Egypt independent and nearly succeeded. The part of Alexandria where she lived and died is now under the sea. Marine archaeologists have recently found her palace and they may soon find her tomb.

Clothes

Like other prehistoric peoples, the first Egyptians probably wore the skins of the

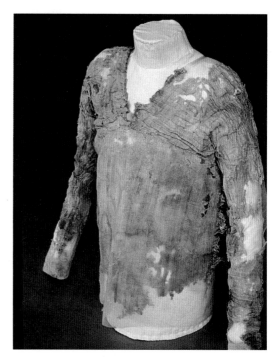

This linen dress is the oldest known dress in the world, dating from about 2800 BC. It was made for a teenage girl.

A coin showing the head of Cleopatra VII.

animals they hunted. By **Predynastic** times, however, they had learned to weave cloth from wool and plant fibres. The most common cloth was **linen**, made from flax, but even this was expensive, so great care was taken not to waste any.

In the **Old Kingdom** clothes were simple, and rich and poor people dressed in much the same way. Men wore a short kilt around their hips, while women wore a long straight dress with shoulder straps or long sleeves. The sleeves were separate pieces that could be sewn on in the winter and taken off in the summer. Although some coloured cloth was made, bleached linen was the most popular material for clothes.

By the **New Kingdom** the upper classes were wearing garments made of cloth so fine that their skin showed through it. Men often wore a short T-shaped tunic under a long pleated kilt, while women wore a large fringed and pleated shawl that was wrapped around the body and tied under the bust to create an elegant draped effect. Young children went naked but older ones dressed like their parents. In cold weather people wrapped themselves in warm cloaks of wool or heavy linen. Underwear for both sexes was a simple linen loincloth. On their feet people wore sandals made from leather, **papyrus** or woven palm fronds.

Special types of clothing were linked with different jobs and classes. The king was often shown wearing a traditional kilt and a variety of **crowns** and headdresses. His **vizier** wore a long robe fastened around the neck with a double strap, while senior **priests** wore long white kilts and white sandals. New fashions began to appear as foreign influences grew in Egypt from the **Late Period**, and by Ptolemaic times **Greek** and **Roman** styles of clothing had been adopted, at least in the cities.

Old Kingdom clothes. The man wears a simple linen kilt, the woman a plain shift dress.

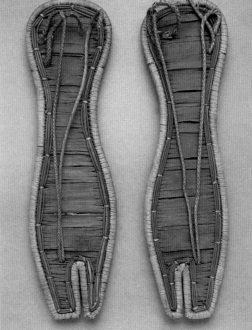

Palm-leaf sandals.

Coffins

The earliest Egyptians were buried in shallow graves in the sand without any kind of coffin. This simple type of burial was all that poor people could expect throughout Egyptian history. Later, wealthy people were buried in coffins, probably to stop wild animals digging up the bodies. The body or **mummy** was wrapped in **linen** and placed inside one or more coffins. The outer coffin is often called a sarcophagus.

Over the centuries many different materials were used to make coffins. The earliest coffins are made of basketwork or wood. The best wood was cedar from Lebanon, which has a pleasant scent that repels most wood- and cloth-eating insects. Cedar was expensive, however, and cheaper coffins had to be put together from small pieces of wood cut from native **trees**. These were sometimes painted red to look like cedar. Pottery coffins have been found in some of the damp **cemeteries** of the Delta. Some outer coffins were carved in **stone** and could weigh several tonnes. A material called **cartonnage** was used for whole coffins or for masks covering the head of the mummy. Some royal coffins were gilded or even made of **gold** or silver.

Many **Old Kingdom** coffins were shaped like houses or palaces because people thought of them as the place where the dead person would live in the **afterlife**. A pair of eyes was often painted on the east side of the coffin so that the dead could see out. During the **Middle Kingdom** rectangular wooden coffins were decorated with pictures of everything the dead person might need in the afterlife. Some coffins even have maps of the next world on them. Another way to help the dead person through the dangers of the afterlife was to write spells on the inside of the coffin. These spells are known as the Coffin Texts. They have titles such as 'Spell for not rotting and for not doing any work in the kingdom of the dead'.

'Anthropoid' (human-shaped) coffins were introduced around the 18th century BC and remained popular for about 2,000 years. The original idea was that a coffin shaped like a person could act as the body of the dead person if the mummy itself was damaged or destroyed. Later coffins of this type were designed to look like **Osiris**, the god who rose from the dead. Anthropoid coffins are often beautifully painted with symbols and images of many protective gods.

*An anthropoid coffin. The shoulders are covered with intricately painted garlands of **flowers**.*

*A painted wooden coffin made during the **Middle Kingdom**.*

Colossi of Memnon

These two enormous statues of King **Amenhotep III** now stand alone in a field, but they once marked the entrance to his memorial temple on the west bank of the River Nile at **Thebes**. There was

The Colossi of Memnon. The figure on the right is the one that used to sing.

nothing unusual about the statues until they were damaged by an earthquake in 27 BC. After this happened, the northern statue began to make strange sounds each morning. This 'singing' attracted crowds of **Greek** and **Roman** visitors, who called the statue Memnon, after the son of Eos, the Greek goddess of dawn. It became so famous that in the 3rd century AD the Roman emperor Septimius Severus decided to have it repaired. Unfortunately, this stopped the singing. 'Memnon' has remained silent ever since.

Copts

Copts are Egyptian Christians. The Bible says that Jesus spent part of his childhood in Egypt in order to escape from King Herod. It was probably St Mark who brought Christianity to Egypt in the 1st century AD, when Egypt was part of the Roman Empire (see **Graeco-Roman Period**). By the 3rd century AD, Christians were translating parts of the Bible into the Coptic language, which had developed from ancient Egyptian. Before

Christianity became the official religion of the Roman Empire, thousands of Egyptian Christians were killed on orders from Rome. Once Christianity had been adopted throughout the empire, some pagan Egyptian temples were turned into churches or monasteries. The rest were left to fall into ruins, or were lived in by poor families. The faces of the old gods were sometimes hammered out.

Many of the early Christians lived as solitary monks in the desert. The most famous Egyptian saints are St Antony, who was haunted by visions of demons, and St Athanasius, who wrote the creed that is still used by many churches. Coptic art is famous for its wonderful textiles. Coptic paintings of the Virgin Mary and baby Jesus may be based on earlier images of the goddess **Isis** and her son. The Copts loved to tell stories about Jesus's childhood in Egypt. Many wells and trees in Lower Egypt are said to have been visited by the Holy Family. Christian Egypt became part of the Byzantine Empire, ruled first from Italy and later from Constantinople. Many great monasteries were built during the Byzantine Period. In the 7th century AD the Arabs conquered Egypt and made it into a Muslim country, but the Christian Copts rarely married Muslims and tended to live in their own villages. The Coptic language is still used in church services. A few monasteries and convents remain and the Copts elect their own Pope.

A colourful textile woven in the Coptic Period.

A **New Kingdom** noblewoman wearing make-up and an elaborate wig.

Cosmetics

The first use of make-up in ancient Egypt was probably practical rather than cosmetic. **Stone** palettes for grinding eye paint were among the first things that prehistoric Egyptians placed in their tombs. It is likely that hunters painted their eyes to help shield them from the fierce glare of the sun shining on the desert sands. They may also have thought that the paint was good for their eyes or gave them **magical** protection. The palettes were often made in the shape of the animals the hunters chased. Green malachite or black lead ore was ground into a powder, mixed to a paste with water and then painted around the eyes.

The later Egyptians, especially the rich, were much more vain. Both men and women wore eyepaint, and took care to protect their skins from the sun with moisturizing ointments. Wealthy ladies also used lipstick and rouge made from red earth. They wore elaborate wigs and dyed their **hair** with powder made from leaves of the henna plant. Cosmetics were highly valued. In wealthy homes they were kept in elegant containers that were often carved in the shape of animals, plants or beautiful young girls.

*Cosmetic equipment, including an alabaster ointment jar and a polished bronze mirror. The mirror handle is decorated with the face of **Hathor**, goddess of love and beauty.*

Creation myths

The ancient Egyptians probably told more stories about the creation of the world than any other people. The priests of every major Egyptian temple produced their own creation myth. Among the gods credited with creating the world are **Amun**-Ra, Aten, **Atum**, **Khnum**, **Neith**, **Ptah**, **Ra**,

Sobek and **Thoth**. The Egyptians were fascinated by the idea of the 'First Time'. All the myths agree that before the First Time there was nothing but a dark watery chaos. Then the spirit of the creator became conscious in the waters of chaos.

There were many different stories about what happened next. One says that a giant blue lotus flower rose above the surface of the water. As its petals opened the world was filled with light and scent for the first time. At the centre of the lotus was the sun god in the form of a naked child. This image was popular in Egyptian **art**. In another myth a small hill known as the Primeval Mound was the first thing to rise above the water. Every major temple claimed that their sanctuary was built on this Primeval Mound. Life began when a golden bird landed on the mound and its cry of joy at finding land was the first sound ever made. In another version the first sound was the honking of the Primeval Goose as it laid the world egg. The creator hatched from this egg and the two halves of the shell became the earth and the sky.

A complicated myth from **Hermopolis** told of the eight oldest beings in the universe – the 'Ogdoad of Hermopolis' – who were the deities of darkness, watery chaos, invisible power and boundless energy. They were shown as frogs and snakes but they came together to form the 'Island of Flame' on which the creator sun god was born.

One of the earliest creation myths came from the temple of the sun god at **Heliopolis**. This told how the oldest being was Atum-Ra. Before the sky and the earth were divided, Atum-Ra 'sneezed out' the god Shu and 'spat out' the goddess Tefnut. This was the beginning of all creatures being divided into male and female. The first people were said to have come from the tears of Atum-Ra.

It was normal for brothers and sisters to mate in the world of the deities. The children of Shu and Tefnut were the earth god Geb and the sky goddess **Nut**. Geb and Nut were passionately in love and they clung together so closely that their father Shu had to force them apart. Only then was there room for Nut's children to be born. In some versions of the story Nut has four children: **Osiris**, **Isis**, **Seth** and **Nephthys**. In others there is also a fifth child, **Horus** the Elder. The nine related deities – Atum-Ra, Shu, Tefnut, Geb, Nut, Osiris, Isis, Seth and Nephthys – were known as the Ennead of Heliopolis.

A much simpler myth from **Memphis** describes how the god Ptah created gods, people and animals by 'the thoughts of his heart and the words of his mouth'.

All these myths agreed that a loving creator had made a perfect world and that it was important for humanity to try to keep everything as it was 'in the First Time'.

Most Egyptian creation myths were also destruction myths. The waters of chaos still surrounded the known world. When life began, chaos monsters such as **Apophis** were formed. The forces of chaos constantly tried to destroy the divine order made by the creator. The gods fought a nightly battle against these forces. The Egyptians feared that one day the creator would become too tired to go on and the whole world would sink back into the waters of chaos. It was the duty of every Egyptian, in life and death, to fight chaos and put off the end of the world for as long as possible.

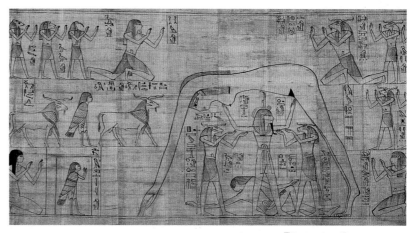

*This **papyrus** illustrates a creation myth. The air god is shown separating the sky goddess from the earth god, so that life can begin in the space between them.*

Papyrus painting from the **Book of the Dead**. *Four baboons guard the Lake of Fire in which the enemies of* **Ra** *were burned.*

Crime and punishment

Most ancient Egyptians feared and respected the law, but some crimes were committed nevertheless. Corrupt priests and officials often abused their power by stealing state property, accepting bribes or exploiting the people who worked for them. Among the citizens, fighting and drunkenness were common, and policemen with dogs were needed to maintain order. People often accused their neighbours and workmates of stealing small items such as clothes or tools. Burglary was one of the commonest crimes, despite strong security in houses. One burglar's confession describes how he took all his clothes off and covered his body in oil in order to wriggle through a tiny window! Thieves were usually fined, and they were sometimes beaten as well. Stealing from temples was a more serious offence because the Egyptians feared that this would make the gods angry.

Crimes against the state, such as running away from military service, were also severely punished. People who disagreed with the government risked being forced to live in one of the remote **oases** of the Western Desert. The only safe way to cross the desert was to join an official donkey caravan, so it was almost impossible to escape from these oases. The Egyptians don't seem to have had long-term prisons; criminals were sent to labour camps instead. The prisoners in these camps were forced to work for the state, digging canals or dragging stone slabs to building sites. The worst punishment was to be made to work in the unbearable heat of the gold mines of **Nubia**.

Corrupt officials who took bribes sometimes had their ears and noses cut off. This happened to some of the judges in a royal murder case, when a queen, a prince and several court ladies were accused of conspiring to murder King **Rameses III**. After the first group of judges had been replaced, most of the accused were found guilty and told to kill themselves. The death penalty was quite rare but it was sometimes enforced for crimes against the dead because stealing someone's burial goods or damaging the **mummy** meant that the person's spirit might not survive. The official penalty for destroying a tomb was to be burnt alive and thieves caught robbing royal tombs were impaled on sharp stakes and left to die slowly. Even so, plenty of people took the risk (see **Tomb robbers**).

Most ancient Egyptians believed that even if you got away with a crime during your lifetime, punishment would catch up with you in the **afterlife**. The dead had to swear before the judges of the underworld that they had never killed or hurt anyone, robbed the poor or stolen anything that belonged to a god. One chapter in the **Book of the Dead** contains a list of forty-two crimes. Among them are gossiping, changing the course of a canal, and winking at the cat goddess. Spirits found guilty of being 'enemies of **Ra**' were boiled in a cauldron or burned in a lake of fire.

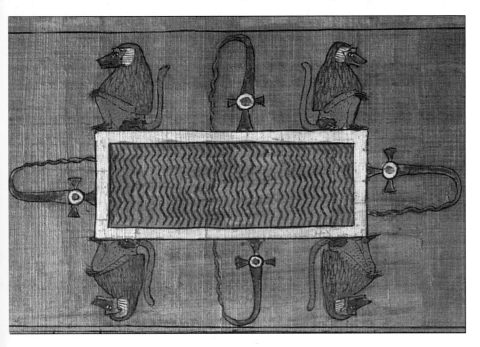

Crowns

Egyptian **kings** wore a range of royal headdresses or crowns. Putting one of these on transformed the king into a god. The most important crowns were the White Crown of Upper Egypt and the Red Crown of Lower Egypt. In reliefs and paintings the king is often shown wearing the White Crown inside the Red Crown (the Double Crown) as a symbol that north and south Egypt were united under one ruler. No examples of the White or Red Crowns have ever been found, but they were probably made of cloth stretched over a light frame. We do know that the crowns had their own **servants** to look after them. From the **New Kingdom** onwards kings also wore the Blue Crown, which was like a helmet covered with gold discs. This is sometimes called the 'war crown', but it was not worn only in battle.

A more informal royal headdress was the *nemes* – the type seen on the famous gold mask of **Tutankhamun**. This was made of striped cloth and usually had a **uraeus** (a representation of a cobra) fastened to the front. Its shape may come from an image of the god **Horus** as the sky-falcon, enfolding the king in his wings. In life only the king could wear the *nemes*, but at some periods non-royal dead were allowed to have this headdress on **coffins** or **mummy** masks.

Egyptian kings also wore circlets made of precious metals, which were more like European crowns. The only crown found in the tomb of Tutankhamun was a gold diadem inlaid with carnelian, turquoise and lapis lazuli. It has gold streamers falling from the back, and a vulture head and cobra at the front. This headdress would have placed the young king under the protection of the goddesses known as the **Two Ladies**. **Queens** wore crowns that linked them with goddesses. Chief queens seem to have a vulture sitting on their head. This was the symbol of Mut, the queen of the

An Egyptian king wearing the nemes *headdress.*

gods. A circlet with two tall plumes transformed a queen or princess into a form of the goddess **Hathor**.

Some gods, including **Atum** and Horus, were often shown wearing the Double Crown because the Egyptians believed that these gods had been rulers of Egypt in prehistoric times. As king of the dead, the god **Osiris** wore the *atef* crown, a tall head-dress with feathers and horns. Kings are sometimes shown wearing this crown. They probably never wore it while alive but after death each king 'joined with Osiris'.

Egyptian crowns

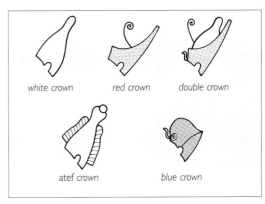

white crown | red crown | double crown

atef crown | blue crown

D

Dancers performing at a party. Dancers wore very few clothes, in order to show off their movements.

This beaded dress was probably worn by a dancer. It would have rattled as she moved.

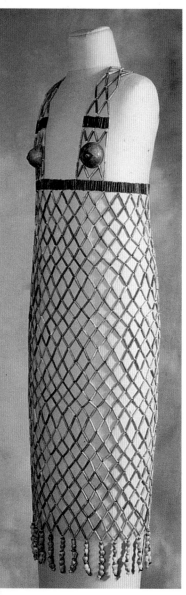

Dance

The ancient Egyptians loved to party, and many of their wall carvings and paintings show happy scenes of **music**, singing and dancing. Athletic young dancers are shown clapping along to the rhythm of music from flutes, harps and lutes while performing acrobatic dances. It is hard for us to know now exactly what their dances were like, but the scenes show them hopping, skipping, twisting, high-kicking and even doing backflips and cartwheels.

Acrobatic dances performed by men and women.

Professional dancers were usually women, though there were male dancers too. Dancers were entertainers but they also played an important part in temple rituals and even **funerals**, where their lively dances may have stood for the dead person's rebirth into a new life.

Deir el-Bahri

Deir el-Bahri lies on the west bank of the Nile at **Thebes**. The first building there was the temple-tomb of King Nebhepetra Mentuhotep, but today Deir el-Bahri is best known for the spectacular memorial temple of the New Kingdom queen **Hatshepsut**. The unusual design was the idea of her architect Senenmut, who was also tutor to her daughter (see **Children**).

Deir el-Bahri.

Deir el-Medina

The ancient village of Deir el-Medina on the west bank of the Nile at **Thebes** is one of the most important sites in Egypt, not because it contains any really spectacular buildings but because the finds made there tell us so much about the way in which ordinary Egyptians lived. Hidden away in a desert valley, the village was built in the **New Kingdom** to house the artists and craftsmen who worked on the royal tombs in the **Valley of the Kings** and **Valley of the Queens**. It was inhabited for nearly 400 years and became a real community, with up to seventy **families** living there at one time. Its remote location meant that everything the villagers needed had to be brought to them, including their clothes, food and drinking water. They even had their own temples to worship the gods, and when they died they were buried in beautiful **tombs** cut into the side of the valley.

Deir el-Medina: the main street.

In the late 20th **Dynasty** attacks by Libyan bandits (see **Egypt's neighbours**) made life in the village too dangerous and it was finally abandoned. The workmen moved to safer homes inside the temple walls at **Medinet Habu**. They left behind their homes and temples, their ancestors' tombs and thousands of documents including letters, poems, stories, work and court records, cartoons and sketches, even laundry lists! These writings and drawings, together with the buildings and objects found in the village, give us a close-up glimpse of what everyday life was like for ordinary people in ancient Egypt.

Demotic

A kind of ancient Egyptian writing (see **Hieroglyphs and writing**).

Dendera

The temple of Dendera in Upper Egypt was the main shrine of **Hathor**, the goddess of love and beauty. The present building dates from the **Graeco-Roman Period** and is known for its beautiful carvings. These include a famous **zodiac** ceiling, which is now in the Louvre museum in Paris.

Diplomacy

Egypt's wealth depended on **trade**, so it was important for the Egyptians to stay on good terms with nearby nations (see **Egypt's neighbours**). Although the rulers of different states sometimes visited each other for talks, this work was usually left to the diplomats – high officials who travelled between courts working out peace treaties and trade agreements. If a state was small or weak, Egypt could offer it military protection in exchange for trading rights or tribute, but a stronger country might demand payment in return for its support. Kings often sealed deals like these with the exchange of extravagant gifts. Sometimes marriages were arranged between the royal families as a way of guaranteeing future peace.

Being a diplomat was an exciting and glamorous job involving lots of travel and the chance to become very rich, but journeying to strange lands could be dangerous. Diplomats and messengers carried government 'passports' proving that they were on state business and promising them safe passage. Passports and diplomatic **letters** were written on clay tablets in the Akkadian language, which was understood throughout the ancient Near East. When these letters arrived at the Egyptian court, the king's **scribes** translated them into Egyptian and then filed them away. A large archive of these letters was found at **Amarna** in the 19th century and examples can be seen in museums all over the world.

*Paying tribute. Near Eastern diplomats present **gold** and silver vessels to the Egyptian king in return for Egypt's protection.*

Doctors and medicine

Egyptian doctors were famous in the ancient world for their skill and knowledge. People could study medicine in temple libraries but they were not allowed to learn by cutting up human bodies. Some **scribes** were part-time doctors and the priests of the goddess **Sekhmet** also treated the sick. Doctors were usually male, but we know of one woman who was an 'overseer of female doctors'. Some doctors specialized in treating certain parts of the body such as the eyes, the stomach, or even the nose. The world's earliest known doctor is a man called Hesyra, who was chief doctor and dentist to King **Zoser** in the 27th century BC. The carved wooden panels from his splendid tomb are masterpieces of Egyptian **art**.

About fifteen medical texts survive from ancient Egypt. Some of these describe the symptoms of various diseases as well as the treatments that were given. The Edwin Smith Papyrus, which dates from around the 16th century BC, divides cases into three types – those that were easy to treat, those that were difficult to treat, and cases that were impossible to treat. One example that is given of the third type of case is clearly a description of angina, a serious heart disease.

Egyptian doctors knew how to set broken or dislocated bones and were able to perform simple surgery, such as lancing an abscess, using reed or flint knives. There were no pharmacies, so doctors had to make the medicines they used from ingredients such as plants and crushed-up minerals mixed with liquids or oils. A typical prescription reads: 'A remedy to calm a cough. Yoghurt and cumin seeds mixed with honey, to be eaten by the patient four days running.' A cure for a skin problem reads: 'If you take baked cucumber and grind it with

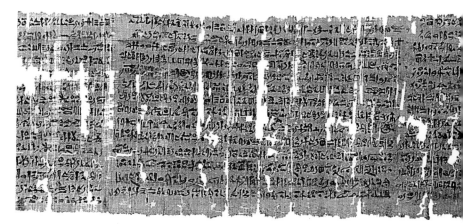

A medical text used by an Egyptian doctor.

aloe vera, add wine and anoint the sore parts, they will heal.' Cucumber and aloe vera are still used in **cosmetics** to soothe the skin. Some Egyptian remedies had very odd ingredients, such as pigs' teeth or crocodile dung. Doctors also used **amulets** and spells to try to improve their patients' health.

Dogs

Dogs were popular pets in ancient Egypt, but they usually had to earn their keep by hunting, herding animals or acting as guard dogs. Common breeds included fast hunting dogs such as greyhounds, and the fiercer mastiffs, which made good watchdogs. Favourite dogs wore leather collars and were given names like 'Woofer' and 'Lively'. They often appear with their owners in tomb paintings and carvings, and were sometimes buried beside them in the same tomb. Some dogs were treated as the **sacred animals** of the jackal god **Anubis**. After they died they were mummified (see **Mummies**) and buried in special **cemeteries**.

The hieroglyphs written above this dog spell out his name, Ankhu, which means 'Lively'.

Dreams

The ancient Egyptians believed that when you were asleep your soul could enter the world of gods and spirits. **Magic** symbols were carved on beds and head-rests to protect sleepers during this dangerous journey. Black magic was sometimes used to send people nightmares, which was very cruel because the Egyptians thought that dreams could foretell the future. Books described common dreams and explained what they meant. It was lucky to dream about eating crocodile meat, but to dream that you were drinking warm beer meant that something bad was going to happen.

People sometimes spent the night in a temple, hoping for a helpful dream. Other people tried to make gods come to them by casting spells. If you wanted to summon the dwarf-god **Bes**, you had to draw his picture on your hand and recite some magic words. The spell warns that if the god speaks, you must write down his words straight away, otherwise the memory will vanish like a dream.

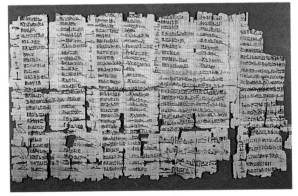

Part of a book of dream interpretations.

Dynasty

The ancient Egyptians divided their **kings** into families that we call dynasties. A history of **Egypt** written by Manetho in the 3rd century BC listed thirty-one dynasties of kings. The beginning of the 1st Dynasty is usually dated to around 3100 BC and the last native Egyptian king was over-thrown in 343 BC. The time between these two dates is often called the Pharaonic Period. **Egyptologists** have divided this huge timespan into Periods and Kingdoms. In books, Egyptian buildings or objects are often said to be of a particular dynasty. This means that they were made during the reign of one of the rulers of that dynasty.

Lists of kings were kept in **temples** so that prayers could be said for all the past rulers of Egypt. The most complete list ever found is a **papyrus** scroll known as the Turin Canon, which gives the names of about 300 kings and the number of years each of them ruled. The Turin Canon was in good condition when it was found in the early 19th century, but a rough ride on the back of a donkey shook it to pieces. Scholars have been trying to put the pieces back together ever since.

Most of these lists of kings miss out the names of unpopular rulers such as **Akhenaten**. They also make it look as if each dynasty followed the next, although during some periods there were several dynasties ruling in different parts of Egypt at the same time. Most dynasties were made up of a series of related kings and a new royal family usually meant the start of a new dynasty. Moving to a new capital city or some other major change in royal policy also sometimes counted as a change of dynasty.

*A list of kings from a temple wall. The kings' names are written inside **cartouches**.*

Early Dynastic Period
(c.3100–2686 BC)

Many of the ideas that made Egyptian civilization unique date to the Early Dynastic Period (1st–2nd Dynasties). At this time, the king became all-important in **government** and religion. Large mud-brick **temples** and **tombs** began to be built, the rules of Egyptian **art** were thought out, and the first **stone** statues of **kings** and **gods** were carved. Hieroglyphic writing was invented and used to record the names and deeds of kings (see **Hieroglyphs and writing**).

Ancient historians believed that the first ruler of all Egypt was a king called Menes, who founded the city of **Memphis** and was later killed during a hippopotamus hunt. Modern historians think that the legend of Menes may be based on the achievements of two real kings, Narmer and Aha. A slate palette (see **Predynastic Period**) shows King Narmer defeating his enemies. On one side of the palette he is shown wearing the White Crown of Upper Egypt and on the other

he wears the Red Crown of Lower Egypt (see **Crowns**). This famous object was found in the temple of the falcon god **Horus** in the southern city of Hierakonpolis.

The kings of the 1st **Dynasty** wrote their names inside a *serekh*, a drawing of a palace with a falcon perched on top. A major civil war seems to have been fought during the 2nd Dynasty, between one king who worshipped the god **Seth** and another who worshipped Horus. The 'Horus king', Khasekhemwy, won. An inscription on his statue states that 47,209 'northern enemies' were killed in the war.

Large tombs were built for important men and women during the Early Dynastic Period. Most 1st and 2nd Dynasty kings and **queens** were buried in tombs at **Abydos** in Upper Egypt. Fragments of furniture and jewellery hint at the treasures they must once have contained. Around some royal tombs many humble burials took place. The people in these graves were probably killed so that they could go on serving their rulers in the **afterlife**. This cruel custom had died out by the end of the 2nd Dynasty.

*A **stela** from a royal tomb of the 1st Dynasty.*

E

A statue of King Khasekhemwy. His enemies are shown being crushed beneath his feet.

The Temple of Horus at Edfu.

Edfu

The temple of the god **Horus** at Edfu in southern Egypt was built by the **Ptolemies** and is the best preserved temple in all Egypt. It is also one of the biggest – its massive **pylon** is 35 m (105 ft) high. Some of the most interesting carvings inside the temple show the **festivals** that were staged there each year, including a visit from the goddess **Hathor** and a play acting out the battle between Horus and his wicked uncle, **Seth**.

Education

Education was highly valued in ancient Egypt but it was only for boys. Some girls may have learned to read and write, but their main role was to stay at home and help their mothers. Being able to read and write was the key to getting a good job as a **scribe**, so parents tried hard to send their sons to school. Education was expensive and not all families could afford it. Boys who did not go to school were expected to work. They had a practical education, often learning the family trade by helping older relatives and copying what they did.

Schools were part of the **temples** and **government** offices where the pupils would work when they grew up. Royal children had their own school in the palace, and the sons of foreign kings were sometimes sent to study at the Egyptian court.

Boys started school at about five years old. The first thing they were taught was how to write the hieratic script used for official documents (see **Hieroglyphs and writing**). They were not allowed to write on **papyrus**, which was too valuable, but used wooden boards, scraps of broken **pottery** or flakes of **stone**. Pupils made their own reed brushes and ground up colours to mix with water and make ink. They had to copy out long, boring lists of words and phrases until they could write them perfectly. Once they could manage this they were allowed to copy whole texts. These texts were usually full of advice about how to behave and were meant to make sure the boys would grow up to be dutiful civil servants.

Older students learned to draw the beautiful hieroglyphs used for religious texts and practised writing the kind of official **letters** and business documents they would come across in their working lives. They also studied the **mathematics** needed for keeping accounts and working out **taxes**. Some took specialist subjects such as foreign languages, history,

A schoolboy's text. The teacher's corrections are written at the top.

Students taking dictation from their teacher.

Egypt's natural environment and resources shaped the lives and beliefs of the ancient Egyptians in many important ways, from the **food** they ate and the **clothes** they wore to their **society** and religion. The Greek historian Herodotus, writing in the 5th century BC, called Egypt 'the gift of the river', and it is true that without the Nile people would never have been able to live there. The Nile provided fish to catch, birds and animals to hunt and wild plants to gather. Later people learned to use the rich black earth of its banks to grow crops, make pots and build houses. This fertile land was so precious to the ancient Egyptians that they called their country *Kemet*, the 'Black

geography, astronomy and law. By the time they were teenagers, they would already have begun their careers as apprentices to senior scribes.

Egypt

Egypt lies on the north-eastern coast of Africa, bordered by the Mediterranean Sea to the north, the Red Sea to the east and the Sahara Desert to the south and west. Egypt's modern neighbours are Libya, Israel and Sudan, but in ancient times political frontiers in the region were always changing as rival peoples such as the Hittites, Assyrians and Persians gained and lost territory (see **Egypt's neighbours**).

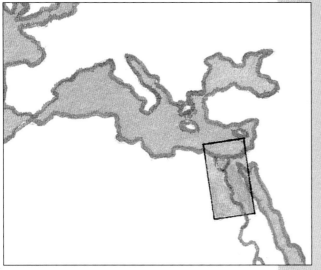

Map of Egypt..

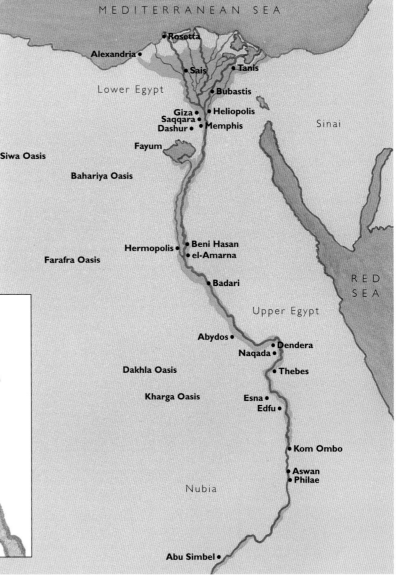

Land', in contrast to *Deshret*, the 'Red Land' or desert, where nothing grew.

The River Nile is almost 7,000 km (4,375 miles) long and is the world's longest river. The ancient Egyptians believed that its source was in a cave beneath Elephantine Island at **Aswan**, but in fact it has several tributaries. The two most important are the White Nile and the Blue Nile. The White Nile begins in Lake Victoria on the borders of Uganda, Kenya and Tanzania and flows all year round. The Blue Nile, which carries away the summer rainfall from the Ethiopian highlands, is full for only part of the time, causing the river to flood each year.

The annual Nile flood was the most important event in the ancient Egyptian calendar, and marked the start of the **year**. As the river rose each summer, its waters spread out across the land, leaving behind a layer of silt washed down on its journey from Ethiopia. The flood waters not only renewed the soil of Egypt's farmlands but were also held back in ponds and reservoirs and used to water the crops all year round.

As the Nile carved its way through the limestone and sandstone rocks of southern Egypt over millions of years, it created a deep valley lined by cliffs. In the north it slowed down on its way to the sea and spread out to create a huge triangular delta. The delta covered 15,000 square km (9,375 square miles). In ancient times these two regions, the Nile Valley, called Upper Egypt, and the Nile Delta, called Lower Egypt, were known as the 'Two Lands'.

The Two Lands were represented by a pair of goddesses known as the **Two Ladies**: Wadjyt, the cobra goddess of Lower Egypt, and Nekhbet, the vulture goddess of Upper Egypt. The idea of the union of the Two Lands was very important to the ancient Egyptians. When Egypt's first kings were looking for a capital they chose a site at **Memphis**, close to where the Nile Valley and the

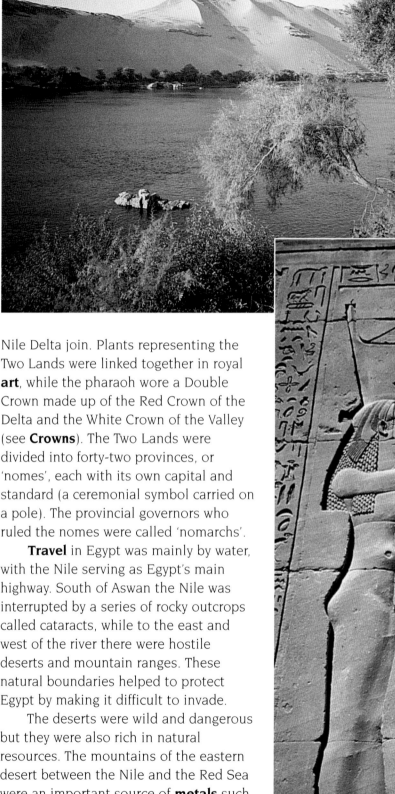

Nile Delta join. Plants representing the Two Lands were linked together in royal **art**, while the pharaoh wore a Double Crown made up of the Red Crown of the Delta and the White Crown of the Valley (see **Crowns**). The Two Lands were divided into forty-two provinces, or 'nomes', each with its own capital and standard (a ceremonial symbol carried on a pole). The provincial governors who ruled the nomes were called 'nomarchs'.

Travel in Egypt was mainly by water, with the Nile serving as Egypt's main highway. South of Aswan the Nile was interrupted by a series of rocky outcrops called cataracts, while to the east and west of the river there were hostile deserts and mountain ranges. These natural boundaries helped to protect Egypt by making it difficult to invade.

The deserts were wild and dangerous but they were also rich in natural resources. The mountains of the eastern desert between the Nile and the Red Sea were an important source of **metals** such as **gold**, copper, lead and tin, semi-precious **stones** such as amethysts and emeralds, and hard building stones such as granite. There were copper and turquoise mines in Sinai, and the **oases** of the western desert were important for growing fruit such as dates and grapes.

The River Nile.

The goddesses Nekhbet and Wadjyt present King Ptolemy VIII with the Double Crown of the Two Lands.

Caravan routes through the deserts also played a part in the trading network that made Egypt rich and powerful (see **Trade**). As well as exporting its own products like grain, **linen** and **papyrus**, Egypt controlled the trade in exotic African goods such as gold, ivory and incense. The country's wealth was one of the main things that tempted foreign powers to occupy Egypt from the **Late Period** onward. Many of the changes the new rulers made were to improve trade: the Persians (see **Egypt's neighbours**) completed a canal linking the Nile with the Red Sea, while the Ptolemaic capital, **Alexandria**, was a busy seaport connecting the Nile with the Mediterranean.

Egypt remained an important centre of trade into the 19th century, when the Suez Canal was built to create a direct route between the Red Sea and the Mediterranean. The major achievement of the 20th century was the construction of the High Dam at Aswan, which has finally tamed the Nile flood, controlling the flow of water so that people are able to grow food all the year round.

Egypt's neighbours

In Egyptian **art** foreigners were usually shown as bound captives or as envoys humbly bringing tribute. In reality, some neighbouring countries were a constant threat to Egypt. Others became trading partners or political allies. To the south of Egypt lay **Nubia**. The Egyptians occupied parts of Nubia so that they could exploit its **gold** mines and control the **trade** routes down into Africa. To the west of Egypt there were nomadic tribes of Libyans, who often raided the western Delta and the **oases**. Many kings sent troops to punish the raiders and Libyan chiefs were sometimes brought back to Egypt to be publicly executed. During the **New Kingdom** thousands of Libyans were taken prisoner and sent to work for **temples**. Many Libyans did well in their new home and their descendants became important **priests** and soldiers. In the **Third Intermediate Period** Libyan families ruled over parts of Egypt.

The Egyptians traded with some of the Mediterranean islands to the north, such as Cyprus and Crete. They also had many trade links with wealthy countries to the east, but relations were not always friendly. Egypt referred to her eastern neighbours as 'miserable Asiatics'. During the **Second Intermediate Period** Egypt was invaded by an eastern people known as the Hyksos. Their name comes from an Egyptian phrase meaning 'rulers of foreign lands'.

The Hyksos made Avaris in the eastern Delta their capital city. Some of the Hyksos leaders took Egyptian royal titles and they worshipped the god **Seth**. For about a century Avaris was a great trading centre and the Hyksos introduced new weapons and craft skills.

The Hyksos were driven out by a new line of Egyptian kings from **Thebes**. These kings and their successors conquered most of Syria-Palestine.

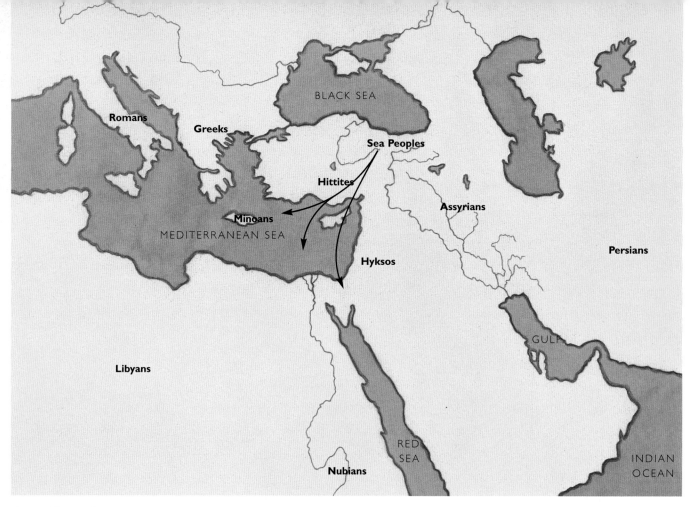

MEDITERRANEAN SEA
BLACK SEA
RED SEA
INDIAN OCEAN

Romans
Greeks
Sea Peoples
Hittites
Minoans
Assyrians
Persians
Hyksos
Libyans
GULF
Nubians

A map of Egypt and its neighbours.

This brought them into conflict with other nations. These conflicts were sometimes resolved by royal marriages or gifts of gold (see **Diplomacy**). The greatest threat came from a warlike people known as the Hittites, who lived in the area that is now Turkey. In the 13th century BC, King **Rameses II** fought a great battle against the Hittites at Qadesh. Later in his reign, Rameses signed a peace treaty with the Hittites and married a Hittite princess.

The peace lasted until the Hittite empire was overrun by the Sea Peoples. This was a mass movement of peoples searching for places to settle. There were at least six different groups, including the Sherden, the Peleset and the Ekwesh. In *c.*1177 BC the Sea Peoples attacked Egypt by land and sea but they were defeated by King **Rameses III**. Many other countries were conquered and resettled by the Sea Peoples. The Sherden gave their name to Sardinia, the Peleset became the

Philistines of the Bible and the Ekwesh may have been the Achaean Greeks who went on to fight the Trojan war.

By the first millennium BC Egypt had dangerous new neighbours. Among them were the Assyrians, an aggressive people from north-east Mesopotamia (modern Iraq). The Assyrians built up a large empire but they were hated for their cruelty by the nations they attacked, such as the kingdoms of **Israel and Judah**. In the 7th century BC the Assyrians invaded Egypt (see **Late Period**) and looted the great temples of Thebes. This act was condemned as barbaric all over the ancient world. The Assyrian empire was eventually taken over by the Persians, whose homeland was northern Iran.

Egypt sided with the **Greeks** against the Persians. This led to a brutal Persian invasion of Egypt. The Persian king, Cambyses, is said to have slaughtered the sacred **Apis bull** and he sent an army to try to destroy the famous temple of the god **Amun** at **Siwa**. The Persians ruled Egypt from 525 to 359 BC and again from 343 to 332 BC. The later Persian kings respected Egyptian culture. They paid for repairs to some temples and even built a new temple for Amun. Egyptian **priests**, **doctors** and artists served at the Persian court. When the Persian empire was defeated by Alexander the Great, Egypt became part of the Greek world (see **Graeco-Roman Period**). By the end of the Ist century BC the Romans had conquered Greece and Egypt. Even after Egypt lost its independence, its art and religion had a great influence on neighbouring cultures.

Egyptology

Egyptology (the study of ancient Egypt) is a lot older than one might think. By the **New Kingdom**, the **pyramids** were already 1,000 years old and the **kings** who had built them were thought of as gods. New Kingdom rulers were fascinated by their ancestors' monuments and liked to show their respect by caring for them. King Thutmose IV left a **stela** recording how he cleared the sand away from the Great **Sphinx** at **Giza**, and one of **Rameses II**'s sons, Khaemwaset, spent much of his career repairing pyramids in the cemeteries of **Memphis**. History was important to the **pharaohs**. As well as recording their own achievements on their monuments, they took an interest in preserving the stories of their ancestors and had lists drawn up showing how they were descended from them. The first proper history of Egypt was written in the 3rd century BC by a priest called Manetho, who divided the kings into thirty-one **dynasties**. This formed the basis of the system Egyptologists use today.

In **Greek** and **Roman** times Egypt was already popular with foreign visitors, who flocked to the tombs and temples, leaving their graffiti all over them.

*The **Rosetta Stone** caused great excitement when it was first displayed at the British Museum in 1803. Its inscriptions were to prove the key to understanding the ancient Egyptian language.*

Classical historians like the Greek writer Herodotus wrote long accounts of their travels in Egypt, in which they tried to make sense of all the stories they had heard and the strange things they had seen. Although not always very accurate, these books were the main source of information about ancient Egypt until European scholars learned to read ancient Egyptian writing in the 19th century (see **Hieroglyphs and writing**).

In the 7th century Egypt was conquered by the Arabs, who were more interested in **trade** than history. Many ancient buildings were pulled down so that new monuments could be built, and the past began to be forgotten. Strange stories grew up around the ancient **tombs** and **temples** and their mysterious hieroglyphs. Medieval European pilgrims visiting Egypt on their way to the Holy Land called the pyramids 'Joseph's Granaries', because they thought they were where **Joseph** had stored up grain during Egypt's years of famine.

In the centuries that followed, many travellers came to wonder at the ancient Egyptian monuments, but it was not until the French emperor Napoleon invaded Egypt in 1798 that any proper scientific study was made. Napoleon's army included a team of artists and engineers who spent four years making a thorough survey of all the monuments in Egypt. This survey was finally published as a twenty-four-volume book called the *Description de l'Egypte* ('Description of

Egypt'). Meanwhile France and Britain were at war. In 1801 the British won the 'Battle of the Nile', a great sea battle off the Egyptian coast. Afterwards many of the ancient Egyptian objects the French had collected were taken as prizes and shipped to England. Among them was the famous **Rosetta Stone**, which the French scholar Jean-François Champollion later used to decode the hieroglyphic script.

In the 19th century Egypt became a magnet for treasure hunters, many of them colourful characters like the Italian circus strongman Giovanni Belzoni. Lots of sites were discovered and excavated at this time, but many of the excavators were only interested in getting objects to sell and anything that could not be sold was just thrown away. Realizing how much vital information was being lost forever, a new generation of Egyptologists, including the Englishman Flinders Petrie and the American George Reisner, began to develop scientific excavation and recording techniques. They understood that knowing where things were found, how they were placed together and how deep they were buried provided vital clues for building up an accurate picture of how the ancient Egyptians lived and died. The methods such men pioneered formed the basis of modern Egyptology.

Many of the objects collected in Egypt during the 19th century found their way into museums such as the British Museum in London, the Musée du Louvre in Paris and the Metropolitan Museum of Art in New York. In 1858, the Frenchman Auguste Mariette started putting together the greatest collection of all in the Egyptian Museum in Cairo. This museum houses some of the most famous ancient Egyptian objects ever found, including the treasures of **Tutankhamun**, excavated from his tomb in the **Valley of the Kings** by Howard Carter in 1922. Today the Egyptian Museum and all the archaeological sites of Egypt are cared for by the Egyptian Antiquities Organization, a department of the Egyptian Government.

Museum conservators clean and restore ancient objects like this mummy mask, and make sure they are kept in the best conditions to preserve them for the future.

Egyptologists still excavate ancient Egyptian sites using traditional techniques, but modern science has given them many new tools. Aerial photography helps in surveying sites and computers are used to keep excavation records and process information. Medical techniques such as X-rays, CAT scanning and DNA testing have been used on **mummies** to learn about sickness and health in ancient Egypt, while chemical analysis of materials can help to reveal where objects come from and how they were made.

Modern Egyptologists have many different kinds of jobs. They work as historians, field archaeologists, epigraphers (people who study inscriptions), scientific researchers, museum curators, papyrologists (people who study papyri – see **Papyrus**), writers, teachers, illustrators or conservators. What they have in common is that they are all working to extend our knowledge of ancient Egypt.

Archaeologists excavating a tomb at Thebes.

Ennead

A group of deities (see **Creation myths**).

Eye of Horus

The Eye of Horus was one of the most common symbols in Egyptian **art**. The god **Horus** could take the form of a giant falcon, whose wings were as wide as the sky and whose eyes were the sun and the moon. The Egyptians told many stories about how the eyes of Horus were damaged in a fight with his wicked uncle, **Seth**. In one version Seth blinded Horus in both eyes, but the injured god was healed with milk by the goddess **Hathor**.

In another version Seth ripped out the left (moon) eye of Horus, then tore the eye apart and threw the pieces into the dark depths of the sea. The wise god **Thoth** used **magic** to find the pieces and join them together again. The restored eye was known as the *wedjat*, the sound or perfect eye. This myth may be based on a lunar eclipse, when darkness seems to gradually destroy the moon. Horus offered the restored eye to his murdered father **Osiris** to help bring him back to life. The *wedjat* was considered sacred and became a symbol of healing and power. It was shown as a human eye combined with the pattern on a falcon's face. The Eye of Horus had its own priests and model *wedjat* eyes were offered to the gods in temples. It became the most common **amulet** to be placed on **mummies**.

A plaque with the sacred Eye of Horus, once used to protect the place on a mummy where the body had been cut open.

Eye of Ra

An Egyptian **creation myth** tells how the first being, the sun god **Atum**-Ra, became lonely and made himself two children called Shu and Tefnut. For a time Atum-Ra and his children were happy together. Then Shu and Tefnut left to explore the limits of their world and were soon lost in the dark waters of chaos. Atum-Ra took one of the eyes from his head and sent it out to find his children. This solar eye lit up the darkness. After a long search, the solar eye found the lost children and brought them safely back. In the meantime Atum-Ra had grown a new eye, and when the first eye saw this it was jealous and became very angry. Atum-Ra transformed the solar eye into a cobra-goddess and placed it on his forehead. Her job was to protect him by spitting fire at his enemies (see **Uraeus**).

This protective goddess was called the 'Eye of Ra'. Many of the goddesses who were daughters of **Ra** had this title. When people or gods did something wrong, the sun god sent the Eye of Ra to punish them. Another myth tells how the Eye goddess quarrelled with her father. She left Egypt and went to live in the **Nubian** desert as a lioness or a wild cat. In one version Atum-Ra sent the hunter god Onuris to catch the Eye goddess and bring her back. In another the wise god **Thoth** lured the angry goddess back to Egypt by telling her interesting stories. This myth was linked to the annual return of the Nile flood (see **Egypt**).

The Eye of Ra was usually shown as part human, part falcon, just like the **Eye of Horus**. The meaning of the two different sacred eyes became confused. Sacred eye amulets were worn to protect, like the Eye of Ra, and to heal, like the Eye of Horus.

The same type of eye as the Eye of Horus – part human, part falcon – could stand for the Eye of Ra.

F

Faience

Egyptian faience is a kind of glazed ceramic material that was used to make bowls, cups, vases and small objects such as **jewellery**, **amulets** and **ushabti** figures. It was made by adding a little lime and ash to ground quartz or sand, then mixing water into this to make a paste that could either be modelled or pressed into clay moulds. Once the pieces were dry they could be painted with glaze and fired in a kiln to give a shiny, brightly coloured surface. Blue and green were the most popular colours for faience, but it was also made in white, purple and yellow.

Blue faience goblet in the shape of a lotus flower.

Family

The family was the centre of ancient Egyptian life, and paintings in tombs often show the different generations enjoying each other's company. The **Old Kingdom** sage Hardjedef advised his readers: 'If you would be a worthy man, set up home and marry a sensible woman, so that a son will be born to you.' People did not expect to live to an old age, so they usually married young and tried to have plenty of children to live after them. When a boy reached adulthood he left his parents'

*An Egyptian family included everyone in the household. This **stela** was made for a man callen Keh, and shows him with his wife, children, servants and other relations.*

house and set up his own home. Girls usually lived with their parents until they married. In the highest levels of **society** marriages were often arranged for political reasons, but generally people chose their partners, and many did marry for love.

Marriage was quite informal – if both families agreed, a couple moved in together. No religious or legal ceremony was required, although from the **Late Period** it was usual to have a marriage contract drawn up in case of arguments about children or property. People often remarried, either because their partner died or because the couple split up. Divorce was quite common and some marriage contracts specify how much a man had to pay his wife if he divorced her. Both men and women left wills to say who should inherit their property.

An ancient Egyptian household could be quite large. As well as the head of the family, his wife and their children, it might include grandparents, unmarried aunts and sisters and, in wealthy homes, **servants** or **slaves**. They all counted as members of the family. The head of the household was always a man, though his wife was known as the 'mistress of the house' and was in charge of running the home. People had great respect for their elders and sometimes kept small figures of dead ancestors in the house. Babies who died were sometimes buried under the floor of the house to keep them close to the family. Some houses had false

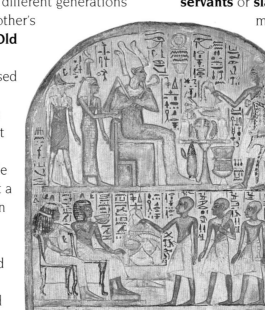

doors (see **Mastaba**) so that the spirits of dead family members could visit.

The whole family shared one living and sleeping space, except in big houses. Apart from this, men and women seem to have led quite separate lives. The man of the house was expected to support his family and usually worked outside the home. **Women** could also work but their first duty was to have babies and look after the house. **Children** usually stayed at home but they were often cared for by nurses and nannies, and sometimes went to live with them. Boys went to school or work as soon as they were old enough (see **Education**), but girls helped their mothers around the house, learning the skills they would use in their own homes.

Farming

Producing enough food for everyone was the most important job in ancient Egypt, and most ordinary people worked on the land for at least part of the year. Much of the farmland belonged to the king and his noblemen, or to big

Farmworkers used wooden hoes to dig the earth.

institutions such as **temples**, which employed stewards to look after their land. The boundaries of fields were marked out with stones to make sure that nobody tried to take someone else's land. Every two years officials measured the fields and checked the stones to make sure there was no cheating and to work out how much of the harvest the landowner would have to pay in **taxes** (see **Weights and measures**).

The most important crops were emmer wheat and barley, which were used to make the basic diet of bread and beer. The next most important were flax for making **linen**, and **papyrus** for making writing sheets. Farmers also grew beans and lentils, vegetables such as onions, cucumbers and lettuces, and fruit such as grapes, dates and figs. In a good year the harvests were big enough to feed everyone and leave some over for export, but in a bad year there were famines and people starved.

Whether a year was good or bad depended on the height of the Nile flood (see **Egypt**). If the flood was too low, there would not be enough water for the crops;

Winnowing. After cereal crops were harvested, they were trampled by animals to separate the stalks from the grain. Then the grain was winnowed, by tossing it in the air so that the wind carried the husks away.

if it was too high, everything would be washed away. As soon as the flood waters had gone down farmers ploughed their land and planted their crops by scattering seeds onto the wet earth, then driving animals over the field to trample them in. The growing plants were irrigated with water held back from the flood or brought from the river using devices like the *shaduf* (water scoop) or the *sakkia* (water wheel). The ripe grain was harvested with a sickle. Flax and papyrus were pulled up by the roots, while fruit and vegetables were gathered by hand.

Most farmers also kept **animals** for food and to help with the work. Tomb paintings often show scenes of oxen pulling ploughs or trampling the harvested grain to separate it from the straw, while trained baboons sometimes helped to pick fruit!

Modern pigeon houses in the Fayum. Ancient Egyptian farmers also kept pigeons to provide food and fertilizer.

Fayum

The Fayum is a fertile region which lies to the west of the River Nile and is connected to it by a natural channel called the Bahr Yusef, or 'Joseph's River', because people once believed it had been built by the Biblical hero (see **Joseph**). The Fayum was one of the first places in Egypt to be settled in prehistoric times and it was still important in the **Graeco-Roman Period**, when big projects for reclaiming the land by channelling the flood water made it even more productive. During Graeco-Roman times the Greek inhabitants of the Fayum adopted Egyptian burial customs and had the bodies of the dead mummified (see **Mummies**), but instead of traditional funeral masks, their faces were covered with lifelike portraits.

These 'Fayum portraits' can be found in museums around the world and are an important source of information on dress, **jewellery** and hairstyles of the time.

Festivals

Many festivals were held in honour of the **gods and goddesses** of ancient Egypt. Calendars marking festival days survive on temple walls and these show that some **temples** celebrated as many as sixty religious holidays a year. During a festival the sacred statue of the god or goddess was taken out of the sanctuary where it was usually kept, placed in a boat-shaped shrine mounted on poles and carried around the temple area on the shoulders of **priests**. It was considered a great honour to 'carry the god'. Some sacred statues even went on long visits to other temples. During the 'Festival of the Beautiful Meeting' a statue of the goddess **Hathor** travelled over 160 km (100 miles) to visit the falcon god of **Edfu**. People would line the riverbank to watch the goddess pass in her boat, 'The Lady of Love'.

On festival days the temple altars were heaped with extra **offerings** of food and drink. These offerings were sometimes shared out later among the crowds who came to the festival. This was the only chance many Egyptians got to taste luxuries like roast beef or wine. At some festivals girls and dwarfs performed **dances** while men competed in **sports** such as wrestling and stick-fighting.

The king and royal family went to the great 'Opet Festival' in **Thebes**, for which

Priests carry a statue of a god through the temple gates during a festival.

images of the gods were taken by boat from the temple of **Karnak** to the temple of Luxor. The procession must have been exciting, with its drummers, dancers and acrobats. The festival of the god **Osiris** was more sombre. It was rather like the Christian festival of Easter. In the fourth month of the year the tragic story of the murder of Osiris was acted out and Egypt went into mourning (see **Abydos**). After several days priests announced that Osiris had risen from the dead and the festival became a celebration. There were also festivals for the dead, when everyone visited their family tombs or graves.

Field of Reeds

The ancient Egyptian paradise (see **Afterlife**).

First Intermediate Period (c.2181–2055 BC)

The troubled era after the end of the **Old Kingdom** is known as the First Intermediate Period (7th–11th **Dynasties**). The royal line of the 6th Dynasty seems to have ended with the death of Queen Nitiqret. The next two dynasties were based at the capital, **Memphis**, but they were not able to control the whole country. The tombs of these 7th and 8th Dynasty rulers are very small in comparison with the huge royal **pyramids** of the Old Kingdom. There seems to have been a shortage of skilled craftsmen during this period.

By the end of the 21st century BC there were rival lines of kings in Upper Egypt at Herakleopolis and **Thebes**. In many areas the real power was held by the nomarchs (governors of a province). Some of these nomarchs had to deal with famines and attacks by neighbouring provinces. The Egyptians looked back on the First Intermediate Period as a time of misery and chaos, when law and order had completely broken down. However, the objects found in First Intermediate Period graves show that many ordinary people were better off than they had been in the Old Kingdom. The wars between rival kings were brought to an end by a Theban, Nebhepetra Mentuhotep, who reunited the country under his strong leadership.

King Nebhepetra Mentuhotep, whose victories ended the divisions of the First Intermediate Period.

Fish and fishing

The plentiful Nile fish were an important protein food, especially for poorer Egyptians, and fishing provided many families with a living. Fishermen caught the fish in nets or traps, or with lines or spears. The Egyptians liked to eat carp, perch and mullet, which was the most expensive – a single mullet was worth a jar of beer. Rich people fished for sport and noblemen liked to amuse themselves by fishing with a rod and line, just like modern anglers.

The easiest way

A painting of fish in a garden pond.

to catch fish was to dig pools and then wait for the Nile flood to fill them. When the waters went down, fish that had been washed into the pools were left stranded and could easily be speared or caught by hand. They were split open and cleaned, then salted or dried in the sun to provide nourishing food for the winter months. Large households made sure of having fresh fish all year round by keeping live fish in their **garden** ponds.

Not everyone ate fish, at least not all the time. Some kinds of fish were not eaten because they were thought to be 'unclean', and **priests** were forbidden to eat fish on certain days. Other types of fish were considered sacred in some places: people from the Upper Egyptian town of Esna never ate the Nile perch, which they worshipped as a form of the goddess **Neith**. Women and children sometimes wore fish-shaped **amulets**, perhaps as **magic** charms against drowning.

Flowers

Garlands and bouquets of flowers often appear in Egyptian **art** as decorations and as **offerings** to gods and the dead. The Egyptians believed that the perfume of flowers came from the gods and contained the power of eternal life, and incense made from flowers was used in **funeral**

Flower headdress from a Roman mummy.

rites and **temple** rituals. **Egyptologists** were able to tell that the young king **Tutankhamun** was buried in springtime because of the flowers found on his body.

In daily life both men and women wore exotic floral **perfumes** made from lilies and lotus flowers, and guests at banquets wore collars and headdresses made of fresh flower petals. Flowers were cultivated in **gardens** and displayed in the home for their beauty and scent. Different flowers had different meanings: the lotus flower was a symbol of rebirth and the emblem of Upper Egypt, while the **papyrus** stood for prosperity and was the emblem of Lower Egypt.

Food and drink

Egypt's fertile soil and abundant wildlife meant that there was usually plenty of food for everyone, except in famine years when the Nile did not rise high enough to water the fields of wheat and barley. These crops were used to make bread and beer, the basic diet of rich and poor alike.

Most people made their own bread and beer at home, but palaces and temples had big kitchens to provide for all the people who lived there. Bread was made by grinding up the grain between two stones, then mixing it into a dough with water, shaping it into loaves and baking these in a clay oven. There were lots of different shapes of bread, and dates or honey were sometimes added to the dough to make sweet cakes. Beer was made at the same time, by adding bits of partly-baked bread to water and leaving it to ferment. When the beer was ready, it was strained into

*Blue **faience** dish painted with lotus flowers and papyrus plants, the symbols of Upper and Lower Egypt..*

*Food **offerings** from tombs, including fruit, berries and flat loaves of bread.*

*New Kingdom tomb painting showing the grape harvest and winemaking. At the top: the harvest. A gardener waters the vines. Below: the grapes are trodden and the juice put into wine jars to ferment. The jars are sealed with mud. In the middle of the lower register: The vineyard's owner makes **offerings** to the harvest goddess Renenutet, shown as a cobra.*

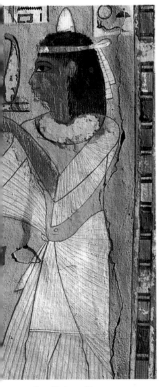

An offering table.

jars. Although there was plenty of fresh water to drink most people seem to have preferred beer!

Rich Egyptians could also drink wine made from grapes, which were first trodden then squeezed in a cloth to extract the juice. Just like modern wine bottles, the wine jars had labels saying where the wine was grown, whose vineyard it came from and when it was made. Drinks were also made from other fruits, and people enjoyed eating fresh and dried fruit including dates, figs and pomegranates.

Salad vegetables included lettuces, cucumbers and spring onions, while peas, beans and lentils could be cooked in stews flavoured with leeks and onions. Herbs like mint, thyme and oregano were also used to add flavour, along with spices such as cumin, coriander

Servants grinding grain and baking bread in pots stacked over a fire.

and aniseed. People also ate almonds and sesame seeds, and sesame and olive oils were used in cooking.

Meat, which was usually roasted over an open fire, was another popular food, though only the wealthy could afford to eat it regularly. Rich Egyptians ate beef, lamb, goat, venison and pork, along with ducks, geese, quail and pigeons. The poor usually had to rely on what they could catch themselves – rabbits, hares and wild birds. **Fish** was also freely available from the Nile. Other animal foods included eggs and dairy products such as milk, yoghurt and cheese.

Except in large households, cooking was the responsibility of the **women** and girls. Part of their job was to prepare packed lunches for the males of the house to take to work or school. When they ate together the family sat around the food and helped themselves, but at large parties, **servants** brought the food and drink round to the guests. Food was served on trays or baskets resting on stands rather than tables. There were no plates, and people ate with their fingers. Drink was served in cups made from pottery, **faience** or even **gold**. Some paintings show party guests feeling ill after eating and drinking too much!

*A mummy is taken to its **tomb** on a sledge drawn by oxen.*

Funerals

In modern Egypt when people die they are buried as quickly as possible. In ancient Egypt things were very different. If the dead person was being mummified, there was a long gap between the death and the burial. Mummification could take up to seventy days (see **Mummies**). There might be an even longer delay if the **tomb** wasn't finished. The mummy was wrapped by the embalmers and placed

*At the tomb, **priests** perform rituals to reanimate the dead person in the **afterlife**.*

inside one or more **coffins**. The coffin seems to have been taken back to the dead person's home so that the funerary procession could start from there. The procession often had to cross the Nile by **boat** to reach a cemetery on the west bank. The coffin was then dragged to the tomb on a sled drawn by oxen.

The **family** walked behind the coffin. Men who were in mourning didn't shave and women often wore headbands of blue cloth. Several kinds of **priest** took part in the funeral. The most important was the lector-priest, who read prayers and spells aloud. Temple dancers sometimes joined in the procession and two women played the roles of the twin goddesses **Isis** and **Nephthys**. These two women sang funeral songs for the dead person, just as the two goddesses had sung laments for their murdered brother **Osiris**. Other women and young girls were hired to weep and wail during the funeral. Tomb paintings show groups of them tossing their hair and beating their foreheads or their chests in grief. The mourners were followed by people carrying the things that were to be buried with the dead person.

When this noisy procession arrived at the tomb the coffin was placed upright. A series of rituals was performed by the priests and by the sons of the dead person. The most important of these were the Opening of the Mouth Ritual and the

Offering Ritual. The Opening of the Mouth Ritual was supposed to restore the mummy's senses so that it could breathe and see and hear again. The same ritual might be used to 'bring alive' a statue of the person who was being buried. In the Offering Ritual the priest read out spells to make sure that the spirit of the dead person would have everything it needed to survive in the **afterlife**. These rituals could go on for days at the funerals of important people. Finally the coffin was left in the burial chamber and the family held a feast in or near the tomb. Afterwards the pots they had used during the meal were smashed. The broken pieces and anything left over from the feast were buried near the tomb. The funeral was not a final goodbye; afterwards, the dead person's family would make regular visits to the tomb (see **Cemeteries**).

Furniture

The ancient Egyptians did not use very much furniture. The rich had beds but most ordinary people slept on mud benches covered with mats. Instead of pillows, there were headrests made of ivory, wood or **pottery**. In wealthy homes there were chairs to sit on, and three-legged stools (which never wobble) were

also popular. Some noblemen even had folding beds and stools to take on hunting expeditions! There were no cupboards or wardrobes; **clothes** and household goods were kept in wooden chests and boxes, while foodstuffs such as oil and grain were stored in pots and baskets. Trays of **food** or jars of drink were put on tall stands.

One reason why furniture was so rare and expensive is that most wood had to be imported from far away – cedar from the Lebanon, ebony from Africa. The Egyptian carpenters became very clever at using wood economically. If you look closely at a piece of Egyptian furniture, you can see that it is made up of many tiny pieces of wood, carefully fitted together. Egyptian furniture was both strong and light because so little wood was used. Pieces made for wealthy customers were often very beautiful, painted or inlaid with ebony, ivory and coloured **stones**. Sometimes the legs and feet of furniture were carved in the shape of lions' paws or bulls' hooves. Royal furniture, covered in gold and set with jewels, was the most extravagant of all.

Furniture like this was made for wealthy homes.

The scribe Nakht and his wife Tjuiu enjoy the cool shade of their garden.

Gardens

The green beauty and cool shade of the garden was a welcome relief from the hot Egyptian sun. Wealthy Egyptians loved to build gardens in the grounds of their houses, filling them with shady **trees**, flower beds, vegetable plots, vine arbours and ponds full of waterlilies where fish and ducks swam. **Temples** also had large gardens tended by armies of gardeners to provide all the **flowers** and plants used in **offerings** and for making the incense and **perfumes** offered to the gods.

Geb

The earth god (see **Creation myths**).

Giza

The Giza plateau in the desert west of modern Cairo was part of the ancient royal cemetery of **Memphis**. Three **Old Kingdom** pharaohs – **Khufu**, his grandson Khafra and his great-grandson Menkaura – built their **pyramids** there. The biggest and most famous of the three is Khufu's Great Pyramid, almost 150 m (450 ft) high, which was built in about 2570 BC. Khafra's pyramid is guarded by the enormous figure of the **Sphinx**, a

mythical animal with a lion's body and the king's head.

Beside the kings' pyramids are the little pyramids belonging to their queens and the **mastaba** tombs of the royal courtiers, arranged neatly in street-like rows. Most of the tombs at Giza were robbed in ancient times but the tomb of Khufu's mother, Queen Hetepheres, was found intact with its beautiful treasures of furniture and jewellery. Among the other discoveries at Giza were some pits containing huge cedar **boats** that might have been used for Khufu's **funeral**.

The Sphinx.

The pyramids at Giza.

One of the boats has been put back together and is displayed in a special museum next to the Great Pyramid.

Glass

Roman glass plaque of the **Eye of Horus**.

Egypt was one of the first civilizations to make glass, and many people think that glass was an ancient Egyptian invention. The idea probably came from the colourful glazes used to decorate **faience**. One of the earliest pieces of glass that can be dated is a little vase decorated with the name of King **Thutmose III**, who lived around 1450 BC. It was made from a mixture of sand, **natron** and colouring, all melted together and shaped around a clay mould. The

*Miniature glass vase. The other side is decorated with the cartouche of King **Thutmose III**.*

same method was used to make bowls, **cosmetic** bottles, beads, **amulets** and coloured inlays for **furniture** and **jewellery**. Transparent blown glass was introduced into Egypt during the **Graeco-Roman Period**, and Egyptian glassmakers became famous throughout the ancient world for their beautiful tableware and cosmetic bottles.

Gods and goddesses

The Egyptian word for 'god' was written with a flagpole sign. Tall flagpoles were set up in front of temple gateways (see **Pylon**) so that the flags fluttering in the wind would make the ancient Egyptians remember the invisible powers that ruled their universe. Hundreds of deities (gods and goddesses) are mentioned in religious writings or shown in religious **art**, but the Egyptians believed that there was one deity who was older and more powerful than all the rest. This was the creator, who had formed the world out of chaos (see **Creation myths**). The creator made numerous gods and goddesses who were worshipped as separate deities, but they also remained part of the creator. The creator was wise, good and immortal. The other deities were not all perfect. They were sometimes cruel or violent and their bodies could be killed.

The most important deities (follow the Gods and Goddesses trail to find them) had their own **temples** and **priests**. These deities were thought to use statues or **sacred animals** as temporary bodies on earth. Priests prayed before the cult statues in temples and made **offerings** to them. Jews and Christians saw this belief as 'idol worship'. To the Egyptians worshipping cult statues was just one way to show respect for the divine order. They also had to please the gods by living good lives and helping others.

Ordinary people sometimes chose one god or goddess to be their patron deity. This might be the deity they were named after (see **Names**), the chief deity of their nearest temple, or one who was relevant to their profession. **Scribes**

often chose **Thoth**, the god who invented writing. The love goddess **Hathor** was particularly popular with **women**. People made regular offerings at the shrine of their patron deity and took a holiday during the deity's annual **festival**. Egyptians on journeys prayed to the gods and goddesses of the places they were

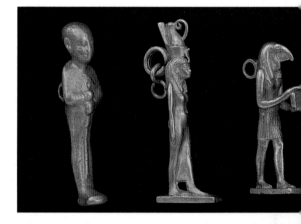

*A row of gods and goddesses on the back wall of the temple of **Dendera**.*

visiting. They were quite happy to recognize foreign deities in the same way.

In some religious writings Egyptian deities were described as vast, shining beings who gave off a wonderful perfume. In art they were often shown as beautiful humans. They were sometimes given turquoise skin and lapis-blue hair to

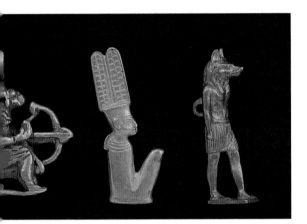

*These miniature figures of deities were once worn as **amulets**.*

distinguish them from people. Gods and goddesses could change their shapes at will and take on animal forms, which helped to express divine powers. The god **Khnum**, for example, had the strength and virility of a ram, while the goddess **Isis** had the motherly tenderness of a cow. Strange half-human, half-animal deities were pictured in temples and **tombs**. Educated Egyptians did not believe that their deities looked like this. It was a way of showing that deities were very different from people or animals and had superhuman powers.

Gold

Gold was a very special and magical material for the Egyptians. It was associated with the sun and with everlasting life, because even if it is buried for thousands of years it still looks new. The Egyptians believed that the bodies of the **gods** were made of gold, and gold masks were used to protect the bodies of dead royalty. The burial

chamber in a royal **tomb** was called the 'House of Gold'. Gold was also important to the pharaohs as a way of keeping the peace with their neighbours (see **Egypt's neighbours**) – by giving lots of gold to the rulers of nearby countries they hoped to make sure that those countries would remain friendly towards Egypt (see **Diplomacy**).

Gold was known and worked in Egypt from **Predynastic** times. Most gold came from the mountains between the River Nile and the Red Sea in southern Egypt and **Nubia**. So much of Egypt's gold came from Nubia that some people think its name originally came from *nub*, the ancient Egyptian word for gold. Mining the gold was very difficult. The mountains were deep in the desert and the only way to get there was on foot or by donkey. Many expeditions had to turn back before everyone died of thirst. Wells were eventually built for the miners, but they still had a hard job cutting out the gold-bearing quartz rock, crushing it and then washing it to get the gold out. Prospecting and mining expeditions were the job of the **army**, and convicted criminals were sometimes sent to the mines as forced labour. The gold was carried back to the cities of the Nile Valley on the backs of porters or donkeys in the form of dust, nuggets or rings. When it arrived it was carefully weighed (see **Weights and measures**), then sent to workshops where the royal goldsmiths turned it into divine statues, **jewellery** and other beautiful objects.

Nubians bringing baskets of gold nuggets and armfuls of gold rings to the Egyptian court.

Government

The government of Egypt was divided between the royal household, the **army**, the priesthood, the foreign service and the civil service, but in practice these quite often overlapped. In many towns the royal palace and government offices were right beside the temple, and soldiers and officials often had part-time jobs as priests. Many of the most important posts were given to the king's sons to train them in government. This meant that the king was surrounded by people he trusted and who would keep him in touch with what was happening in his country. He also had a vast personal staff which included a chancellor, a steward and a chamberlain, plus secretaries, wardrobe keepers, hairdressers and beauticians, cooks and all the rest of the palace **servants**.

After the king, the most important person in Egypt was the **vizier** or prime minister, who was the king's right-hand man and personal adviser. The army and navy were headed by commanders-in-chief. As well as fighting wars and protecting Egypt's borders they had to organize trading and mining expeditions. The priesthood was led by a supreme high priest. His job was to see that the **temples** were properly supplied, maintained and staffed, that **festivals** and rituals were properly carried out, and that any **priests and priestesses** appointed were loyal to the king.

*Government officials were responsible for running the country. They often wore distinctive **clothes** that showed their rank.*

Foreign affairs were managed by the governors of foreign provinces and the diplomatic service (see **Diplomacy**).

Each Egyptian town had its mayor and council, who answered to the central government. The civil service was responsible for the general running of the country, including maintaining **law and order**, collecting **taxes** and paying state employees. There was no money, so people were paid in goods such as grain and oil, which they could then **trade** for other things. All the goods collected in taxes and used to pay people were kept in big stores controlled by officials with grand titles like 'the Overseer of the Granaries of the Two Lands'.

Graeco-Roman Period
(332 BC– AD 395)

In the 4th century BC Egypt was being ruled by the Persians (see **Egypt's neighbours**) until Alexander the Great, the young King of Macedonia in Greece, defeated them and made Egypt part of his empire. Some years after Alexander's death a Greek general called **Ptolemy** took power in Egypt. He was the first of fifteen kings of this name who ruled Egypt from **Alexandria** on the Mediterranean coast.

Under the Ptolemies the government was run by Greeks and very few native Egyptians were given important posts, although the Egyptians were allowed to keep their own **laws** and their own religion. Most of the Ptolemies did not bother to learn the Egyptian language, but they did take part in some Egyptian religious ceremonies. They also introduced the cult of a new god called Serapis, which was designed to appeal to both Greeks and Egyptians. **Priests** were still powerful and respected in Egyptian society. The Graeco-Roman Period **temples** built for Egyptian gods at **Dendera**, **Edfu**, Kom Ombo, and **Philae** are among the greatest ever constructed

in Egypt. **Art** flourished under the Ptolemies, when fine sculpture and exquisite glassware were produced.

The first three Ptolemies were strong kings who made Egypt a great power in the Near East. Later kings were weak and the Ptolemy family began to go from bad to worse. Murderous family feuds and civil wars between rival kings weakened Egypt. The native Egyptians in the south tried to rebel and there were frequent riots in Alexandria. Some of the Ptolemies were foolish enough to ask Rome for help. The **Romans** were keen to rule over Egypt because it was so rich in grain and gold. **Cleopatra VII**, the last Ptolemy queen, used her love affairs with two Roman generals to make Egypt powerful again. She wanted to be 'Queen of Queens' in a new Egyptian empire. Cleopatra was finally defeated by another Roman leader, Octavian, in 30 BC.

Octavian became the Emperor Augustus and Egypt was treated as his property. The Romans imposed their own laws and heavy **taxes**, and a fleet of ships full of Egyptian grain sailed for Italy every year. The Romans did sponsor some **temple**-building in Egypt and **Nubia**.

The temple of Dendur (which was transported to New York in the 1960s) was begun in the reign of Augustus. Augustus is shown on the temple walls, dressed like an Egyptian king and worshipping Egyptian gods. In fact, the Roman Emperors never did this, although a few of them visited Egypt.

Mask from the **coffin** of a woman who lived in Graeco-Roman Egypt. She wears a Greek hairstyle.

The last Roman emperor to appear on the walls of Egyptian temples was Diocletian, who died in AD 305. He was revered by the pagan Egyptians because he tried to stamp out Christianity (see **Copts**). In AD 384 the Christian Emperor Theodosius ordered all the pagan temples of Egypt to close. The temples were the guardians of ancient Egyptian culture and language so this was a major break with the past. The traditional date for the end of the Roman Period is AD 395, when Egypt became part of the Byzantine Empire.

Greeks

Egypt had close contact with the Minoan people of the Greek island of Crete during the 2nd millennium BC. At that time oil, wine and painted pottery were imported from mainland Greece and the islands of the Aegean. In the 7th century BC an Egyptian king allowed Greek traders to settle at Naukratis in the Nile Delta. The silver and bronze coins used in Naukratis were the first coins to be made in Egypt. Some Greeks came to Egypt to serve as mercenary soldiers, while other visitors were interested in its **art**, **architecture**, and religion. Ancient writers say that the Greeks borrowed many ideas from Egypt, and early Greek sculpture was certainly influenced by Egyptian art.

Greek became the official language of **government** in Egypt during the reign of the **Ptolemy** family and most Egyptian towns were given Greek names. Many Greek people came to settle in Egypt. Some chose to worship Egyptian **gods** and follow local burial customs and underground **tombs** in **Alexandria** are decorated in a strange mixture of Greek and Egyptian styles.

If Greeks had never lived in Egypt we would know less about their culture, since some of the great works of Greek literature only survive because they were copied onto **papyrus** and preserved in the dry sands of Egypt. More than 15,000 Greek papyri have been found at the town of Oxyrynchus in the **Fayum**. Scholars have been working for over a century to translate all these papyri.

*Figures wearing Greek dress in an Egyptian **tomb** of the 4th century BC.*

Wig made from human hair.

Wooden comb.

Hair

The Egyptians were very proud of their hair, which they loved to wear in fancy styles. Tomb carvings and paintings from the **Old Kingdom** onwards show both men and women having their hair tended by hairdressers. **Children** often had their heads shaved, sometimes leaving just a single lock known as the 'sidelock of youth'. **Priests** also had to have their heads shaved, and body hair was usually removed. Men were usually clean-shaven, although moustaches and beards were sometimes in fashion and the king wore a false beard as part of his regalia.

The Egyptians used a whole range of preparations to keep their hair looking nice, including conditioners to repair the damage done by the hot sun and setting lotions to hold their elaborate plaits and curls in place. They also liked to colour their hair with dyes – henna, one of their favourites, is still used in many parts of the world to dye hair a rich red colour. Wealthier people could afford wigs made of real human hair, which gave them an instant change of hairstyle.

Children often had their heads partly shaved to keep them cool and discourage head lice.

Hathor

Hathor was one of the most important and best loved of all Egyptian deities. Her name means 'Mansion of Horus'. **Horus** was a falcon god and his mansion was the sky. Like the goddess **Nut**, Hathor could be shown as the sky cow, with starry markings and carrying the sun disc between her long horns. She could also appear as a beautiful woman wearing a sun disc and cow's horns on her head. The Hathor-mask, a flattened human face with the furry ears of a cow, was carved at the top of columns and used to decorate mirror handles (see **Cosmetics**). Hathor also sometimes appeared as a striped and spotted cat.

In Egyptian myth Hathor was the foster-mother of Horus, which made her

In this image of Hathor the face of a beautiful woman is combined with the ears of a cow.

the foster-mother of every Egyptian king. Her milk was said to give the **kings** long life and great power and they are sometimes shown suckling from the udder of the cow goddess. They probably did drink milk from the herds of sacred cows kept at some **temples** of Hathor. People hoped that the goddess would 'mother' them in the **afterlife**. She was one of the main helpers of the dead and she guarded the sun god **Ra** on his nightly journey through the underworld (see **Underworld Books**).

Hathor was also a goddess of love and sex. When the sun god was angry and refused to shine, Hathor lightened his mood by performing a striptease. The **Greeks** identified Hathor with their goddess Aphrodite and the **Romans** identified her with Venus. People asked Hathor for help with their love life and she is often mentioned in love poetry. **Women** prayed to her when they wanted to have a baby. But Hathor was not always gentle and kind – she was one of the goddesses sent out by the sun god to punish his enemies. As the **Eye of Ra** she spat fiery poison like a cobra or killed and ate people like a lioness.

Hatshepsut

Queen Hatshepsut ruled Egypt for over twenty years during the 15th century BC. She is often called the 'only female pharaoh', although there were several others (see **Queens**). Hatshepsut was the daughter of one king and the widow of another. She became queen regent for her young stepson **Thutmose III** in about 1473 BC, but after a few years she stopped calling herself queen regent and had herself crowned 'king'. In **temple** carvings and statues she was often shown as a man, wearing the **clothes** of a king. Hatshepsut claimed that she had always been the rightful heir to the throne and that her real father was the god **Amun**.

Whatever people thought of this story, Hatshepsut's reign was a successful one. Egypt was mainly at peace during this time and trading expeditions were sent as far north as Byblos in Lebanon and as far south as Punt in Africa. Hatshepsut was a great builder and the **art** produced during her reign is very fine. She had four great **obelisks** set up, 'the like of which had never been seen before', and the temple she built at **Deir el-Bahri** is one of the most beautiful in all Egypt. It was probably designed by a man named Senenmut, who was one of Hatshepsut's most favoured officials.

Thutmose III was prevented from holding any real power for more than twenty years. He may eventually have overthrown his stepmother or she may just have died naturally. It is possible that she was never buried in the king's tomb

*Hatshepsut, shown as a man, is crowned by the goddess **Hathor** (and the god **Amun**-Ra).*

This huge statue of the god Thoth as a baboon once stood outside his temple at Hermopolis Magna.

that she had prepared for herself. Some years after Hatshepsut's death Thutmose III tried to erase the memory of her reign by having her name hammered out wherever it appeared. Many statues of her were smashed to pieces. Hatshepsut was usually left out of official lists of Egyptian kings, but since the rediscovery of her temple at Deir el-Bahri she has become one of ancient Egypt's most famous rulers.

Heliopolis

The Egyptian city of On, now a suburb in the north-east of Cairo, was known to the **Greeks** as Heliopolis, 'City of the Sun God'. In ancient times the sun god **Ra** was worshipped there at a huge temple that was said to mark the site where the phoenix first alighted at the beginning of time (see **Creation myths**).

Hermopolis

The ancient town of Hermopolis Magna (modern-day Ashmunein) got its name from the **Greeks**, who thought its chief god **Thoth** was the same as their god Hermes. Thousands of baboons and ibises, Thoth's **sacred animals**, were kept in his temple there and buried nearby in underground catacombs when they died. The ancient Egyptian name for Hermopolis was Khmun, or 'Eight-Town', because the eight mysterious creator **gods and goddesses** who first brought the world into being were worshipped there (see **Creation myths**).

Hieratic

One of the main ancient Egyptian scripts (see **Hieroglyphs and writing**).

Hieroglyphs and writing

Ancient Egyptian is one of the oldest written languages known. It forms part of the Afro-Asiatic family of languages (to which Hebrew, the original language of the Old Testament, also belongs). Writing was first developed in Egypt in the late 4th millennium BC, using a script called hieroglyphics. This is one of the most beautiful forms of writing ever invented and is made up of pictorial signs and symbols known as hieroglyphs. The word 'hieroglyph' comes from Greek and means 'sacred carving', but the Egyptians

Beautifully painted hieroglyphs on a coffin.

themselves called their writing 'the divine words'.

Hieroglyphs are unusual in that some stand for sounds and others for ideas. The basic sound of a word was shown by one symbol, followed by another to explain what sort of word it was. People's **names**, for example, had a picture of a man or a woman at the end. The exact vowel sounds in a word were not written down, and there were no spaces or punctuation marks between words. The hieroglyphic script usually reads from top to bottom and from right to left.

About 700 hieroglyphic signs were in general use for most of Egyptian history. These included twenty-four signs for individual sounds (which may be the distant ancestors of the alphabet that European languages use today). In the **Graeco-Roman Period** the hieroglyphic script was deliberately made more difficult to read and thousands of new signs or meanings were introduced. Hieroglyphs are nearly all images of the creatures, plants and objects that the Egyptians saw around them. Some are easy to recognize, such as the picture of an owl for the *m* sound. Others show only part of an object from a particular angle and these can be harder to interpret. Hieroglyphs could be drawn as simple outlines, but they were often elaborately carved and painted.

The hieroglyphic script was mainly used for royal or religious texts carved in

A picture of an owl was the hieroglyph for the letter M..

Part of the hieroglyphic and demotic inscriptions on the **Rosetta Stone**.

A potsherd with an inscription written in hieratic.

stone or wood. Religious and magical texts were also written in hieroglyphs on **papyrus** or leather scrolls. A simpler version of the script, known as hieratic, was used for legal and business documents, **letters** and **stories**. These kinds of text were normally written in ink with a reed brush on papyrus or pieces of stone or pottery (**ostraca**). In hieratic script, which was also usually written from right to left, the complicated hieroglyphic pictures are reduced to a few strokes and curves. Boys training to be **scribes** learned hieratic first (see **Education**) and only a few advanced students went on to learn hieroglyphs. Most ancient Egyptians could not read the hieroglyphic inscriptions they saw on temple walls or royal statues.

In the 1st millennium BC a new script called demotic began to be used instead of hieratic. Demotic means 'popular script' but can be very hard to read. It is one of the three scripts found on the **Rosetta Stone**. Finally, in about the 1st century BC, the Coptic script was invented (see **Copts**). Coptic, which

gradually replaced all the older scripts, was written with the twenty-four letters of the Greek alphabet and six signs taken from demotic. Coptic was the first Egyptian script in which the five vowels were written out. Scholars use Coptic texts to work out how ancient Egyptian words may have been pronounced.

By the 5th century AD there was probably no one left who could read hieroglyphs. The first person to do so in modern times was the French scholar Jean-François Champollion (see **Egyptology**).

A relief from the temple of Edfu shows Horus (centre) spearing an evil hippopotamus.

Horus

Some of Egypt's earliest deities were falcon (hawk) gods. Horus was the most important of these and the most complicated. He was usually shown as a falcon or a falcon-headed man. At first there seem to have been at least two gods called Horus.

Horus the Elder was one of the five children of the earth god Geb and the sky goddess **Nut** (see **Creation myths**). His wings spanned the sky and his eyes were the Morning and the Evening Stars, or the sun and the moon. Another form of this sky-falcon was Horakhty ('Horus of the Horizon'), the splendour of the morning sun. In **temples** the sun was often shown as a disc with falcon's wings.

Horus the Younger was the son of **Isis** by her dead husband **Osiris**. He was brought up in the marshes to hide him from his wicked uncle **Seth**. Horus was one of the few Egyptian gods who could be shown as a child. The image of 'Horus the Child' trampling on dangerous animals and strangling snakes with his bare hands is found on magical objects (see **Magic**). When he was still a youth

Horus fought his uncle for the throne of Egypt. During one fight the left **Eye of Horus** was torn out by Seth, but it was later healed by the god **Thoth**. This restored eye became one of the most powerful Egyptian symbols. In the end Horus was crowned King of Egypt and carried out rites for his father that helped Osiris to rise again as King of the Dead.

Gradually all these forms of Horus got confused and they were often treated as one god. Each new king of Egypt became a Horus, in the same way that the burial rites turned each dead king into an Osiris. Every king had a 'Horus name'. Early kings wrote their name inside a picture of a palace with a divine falcon perched on top (see **Early Dynastic Period**). Horus was the chief god of many temples, including those at Hierakonpolis ('Hawk Town') and **Edfu**. Live falcons were kept at Edfu and each year one was chosen to play the god.

Houses

Ancient Egyptian houses were built out of mud-brick (see **Building**) then plastered and whitewashed to reflect the sun. The Egyptians built their houses with the walls sloping inwards to make them strong enough to resist floods or earthquakes. Houses had tiny windows to keep them

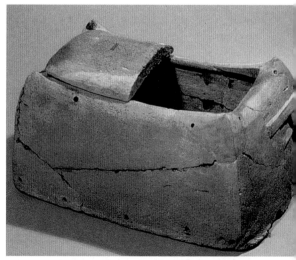

Predynastic model house. Egyptian houses had tiny doors and windows to keep them cool inside.

*The house of the **New Kingdom** scribe Nakht. The triangular shapes on the roof are wind catches to cool the inside of the house.*

cool and shady and to keep burglars out. The homes of wealthier families had their inside walls plastered and decorated with brightly-coloured paintings or hangings. Some even had vents on the roof to send cool breezes through the house – an ancient kind of air conditioning!

Houses in towns were built close together, but in the countryside there was room for people to have **gardens**. There were huge differences between the homes of the rich and the poor. The enormous villas of the rich were set in great estates. They had many rooms, and separate stables, storerooms, workshops and kitchens, while most houses just had a small yard at the back with a clay oven and a grindstone. Wealthy homes even had bathrooms and toilets, but most people had to wash in the river.

Big and small houses had the same kind of layout. There was a reception area at the front, sometimes with a porch. Behind this were the private rooms where members of the family ate and slept. In towns, where ground space was limited, there was often an upper floor, and in hot weather many people slept on the roof. Some houses also had cellars where things were stored for safety. There was very little **furniture** but most houses had built-in benches to sit and sleep on.

*Nebamun and his family hunting in the marshes. The tame goose on the front of the **boat** is acting as a decoy.*

Hunting

The first Egyptians depended on hunting for survival and prehistoric rock drawings show the exotic desert creatures they caught – ostriches, gazelles, even giraffes. Hunting in the desert later became more of a sport for the rich, although ordinary people still hunted birds and small animals for food.

Birds were usually hunted along the riverbanks or in the marshes, where they were trapped in nets or hit with throwing-sticks similar to boomerangs. Hunters had some clever ways of attracting their prey – sometimes a tame goose acted as a decoy, calling wild geese towards the hunter. Hunters used **dogs** and even **cats** to fetch the birds they knocked down with their throwing-sticks. In order to catch birds in a net, the hunters would spread the net out on the ground and bait it with food. Then, when birds came down to feed, men hidden in the tall reeds would pull the net tight, trapping them inside.

Egyptian **art** often shows kings in their chariots hunting wild animals such as lions and wild bulls inside special hunting grounds guarded by soldiers, or trapping birds in nets. These scenes also have another meaning. Wild creatures and the desert were associated with the wicked god **Seth**, so pictures like this were a way of showing the king's power over the forces of evil.

Hypostyle hall

A hall with a roof supported by many decorative columns (see **Temples**).

*The hypostyle hall in the temple of **Khnum** at Esna.*

Imhotep

Imhotep is probably the first genius in history that we know by name. He lived in the 27th century BC and was the **vizier** of King **Zoser**. As the 'Director of Public Works in Upper and Lower Egypt', Imhotep was responsible for designing a huge stepped **pyramid** for his king at **Saqqara**. No previous king had ever had such an impressive tomb. A statue base carved with Imhotep's name and titles was found close to the pyramid. Later Egyptians thought that Imhotep had invented the idea of stone **architecture**. This is not true, but the Step Pyramid is one of the world's great buildings. Imhotep was also famous for his **wisdom**. He is said to have written books, though none of these survive.

Long after his death Imhotep began to be worshipped as a god of wisdom and medicine. A legend sprang up that he was the son of the god **Ptah** by a human mother. We don't know what the real Imhotep looked like, but as a god he was usually shown as a priest holding a book-scroll. Shrines were built for him and people brought **offerings** to the tomb at Saqqara where they thought he was buried. Sick people slept near this tomb or in shrines of Imhotep, hoping that the god would come to them in their sleep and tell them how they could be cured. **Priests** of Imhotep helped people to interpret their **dreams**.

*A bronze figure of Imhotep made about 2,500 years after his death. Figures like these were often placed in **temples** by sick people who wanted Imhotep to cure them.*

Isis

The ancient Egyptians thought of the goddess Isis as the ideal wife and mother, but her story is full of suffering and struggle. She was one of the five children of the earth god Geb and the sky goddess

Faience plaque showing Isis and baby Horus hiding in the marshes.

Nut (see **Creation Myths**) and is said to have fallen in love with her brother **Osiris** in their mother's womb. Osiris and Isis were destined to marry each other and become the first king and queen of **Egypt**. Isis was usually shown as a woman with a throne emblem on her head. She often had bird's wings as well as arms. Her **sacred animals** were the kite (a small bird of prey) and the cow. She also appeared as a cow-headed woman, or wore the sun disc and horned headdress of the cow goddess **Hathor**.

One of the titles for Isis described her as 'Great of Magic'. She was said to be 'more clever than millions of men'. In one myth she tricked the sun god **Ra** into telling her his secret name, which gave her great power, but all her cleverness couldn't save Osiris from his jealous brother **Seth**. Osiris was murdered by Seth, and afterwards Isis and her sister **Nephthys** gathered up the pieces of his broken body and Isis used her **magic** to revive Osiris just long enough for her to conceive his child. Seth then took Isis

prisoner but she escaped and fled to the Delta, where she gave birth to her son **Horus** on a hidden island in the marshes. Many reliefs and figurines show Isis nursing baby Horus.

Seth tried to poison Horus but Isis healed him with her magic powers. When Horus was grown up he challenged Seth

*A bronze and **gold** figurine of Isis and her son Horus.*

for the throne of Egypt and Isis helped her son to defeat his wicked uncle. Horus became king of Egypt and Osiris became king of the underworld. Isis took her place as queen of the underworld. She was an important goddess for royalty because Egyptian kings were identified Horus and, when they died, with Osiris.

During the 1st millennium BC a temple of Isis was built on the island of **Philae** to guard Egypt's southern border. The magic of Isis was thought to be stronger than an army of soldiers. In the **Graeco-Roman Period** Isis the 'All-Loving Mother' became the most popular Egyptian deity. Her main appeal was that she offered the hope of a happy **afterlife**. The **Roman** government tried to ban her worship, but Isis soon had followers all over the Roman Empire. A temple of Isis was found in the ruins of Pompeii and she was worshipped in Roman Britain. Only the rise of Christianity put an end to her reign as 'Queen of the Gods'. Philae was the last of Egypt's pagan temples of to be closed. Today Philae is visited by modern Isis-worshippers from Europe and America.

Israel and Judah

The earliest Egyptian source to name the land of Israel is a **stela** dating to the late 13th century BC, which lists Israel among the lands conquered by King Merenptah, the son of the famous **Rameses II**. For centuries before this the Egyptians had known about nomads called the Aiperu and the Shasu, who may have been Hebrew tribes. The Israelites fought many wars against their neighbours to make their country secure and by the early 10th century BC King Solomon was ruling a strong and independent Israel. He built a magnificent temple in Jerusalem for the god of Israel. Solomon is said to have been the first foreign king to be allowed to marry an Egyptian princess.

But relations between Israel and Egypt were not always friendly. King Shishak, who looted the temple in Jerusalem, was probably Sheshonq I, a ruler of Egypt in the late 10th century BC (see **Third Intermediate Period**). He carried off a huge amount of treasure and possibly even the Ark of the Covenant (the chest containing the laws of the Israelites). By this time part of Israel had become the independent kingdom of Judah. Both kingdoms were threatened by the growing power of the Assyrians (see **Egypt's neighbours)**. Israel was conquered by the Assyrians in about 722 BC.

The kings of Judah made an alliance with Egypt and this led to Egypt being invaded by the Assyrians (see **Late Period**). In the 3rd century BC the Greek kings who were ruling Egypt made Judah part of their empire for a time. By the late 1st millennium BC many displaced Jewish people had settled in Egypt. The largest Jewish colonies were in **Alexandria** and **Aswan**.

*In one of the scenes on this **obelisk** a king of Judah is forced to grovel to the Assyrian king.*

Jewellery

The Egyptians loved to wear jewellery from the earliest times. Simple necklaces and bracelets made of pierced stones and shells have been found at **predynastic** burial sites, and by the time of the **Old Kingdom** royal jewellers were using **gold** and silver set with coloured stones.

By the **New Kingdom** a huge variety of jewellery was worn by both men and women, including necklaces, bracelets and anklets, girdles and hair ornaments, rings and earrings, pendants and wide collars of brightly-coloured glass beads. Pearls were popular in the **Graeco-Roman Period**, and **Cleopatra VII** once famously demonstrated her wealth by dissolving a huge and priceless pearl in a cup of wine and drinking it! Only the wealthy could afford gold and silver, but just about anyone could have some of the colourful jewellery made from **faience**. Even animals wore jewellery – tomb paintings show pet **cats** wearing elegant collars and gold and silver rings in their ears and noses!

Jewellery could be more than just ornamental and many pieces included little images of **gods and goddesses** or **amulets**. Mothers put fish-shaped

Bow drills like this were used for drilling holes in beads.

Goldsmiths and jewellers at work. The men on the left are using bow drills like the one above.

Egyptian jewellers were experts at making beautiful ornaments.

skin' and stank 'more than fish eggs'! People didn't even have much respect for their own colleagues – the artists who worked in the royal tombs in the **Valley of the Kings** often spent their free time drawing unflattering pictures of each other. Like the audiences of modern cartoon films, they were also greatly amused by drawings of animals in ridiculous situations – a hippo sitting in a tree, a lion playing games with a gazelle, or a mouse having its hair done by a cat!

A tomb seems like an odd place to look for humour, but Egyptian tomb paintings are full of comic scenes of daily life – men falling asleep at work, sailors tumbling out of boats into the water, and animals getting up to mischief under their owners' chairs. Sometimes captions written in **hieroglyphs** tell us what people are saying to each other. For example, a brewer interrupted by a child exclaims: 'May you be driven off by a

Sketch of a stonemason from Deir el-Medina. This unflattering portrait was probably drawn by one of his workmates.

amulets in their children's hair to protect them from drowning in the Nile, and special charms and collars were placed on **mummies** to keep them safe on their journey through the afterlife. Kings often used gifts of jewellery to show royal favour: faithful service was rewarded with gold collars (see **Society**), and high officials wore special jewellery as symbols of their rank and authority (see **Maat**).

Jokes

The ancient Egyptians liked to laugh and joke just as much as we do today, although their sense of humour was not always quite the same. **Scribes**, who thought they were much better than everyone else, liked to make fun of other peoples' jobs: according to them the poor metal-worker had fingers 'like crocodile-

Ancient Egyptians liked to laugh at absurd situations, like this cat put in charge of a flock of ducks. But this picture may have another meaning, warning of the danger of giving power to a corrupt official.

hippopotamus!' In another tomb an old man boasts that he can work much harder than the youngsters, who tell him to be quiet and get on with it. Perhaps the events in scenes like these really happened and the tomb-owners wanted to be reminded of them so that they could have a good laugh in the next life!

Joseph

The story of Joseph is found in the Book of Genesis in the Bible. It tells how Joseph was sold into slavery by his brothers and taken to **Egypt**. He became the favourite **slave** of a wealthy Egyptian called Potiphar. Potiphar's wife pretended that Joseph had tried to seduce her and Joseph was thrown into prison, where he impressed the other prisoners by telling them what their dreams meant. The king of Egypt was troubled by a dream in which he saw seven fat cattle followed by seven starved cattle. Joseph warned the king that this meant Egypt would have seven years of good harvests followed by

In the Bible story, Joseph told the ruler of Egypt the meaning of his dreams about cattle.

seven years of famine. The king put Joseph in charge of storing grain. Egypt survived the famine and Joseph was rewarded with power and riches. He is said to have married the daughter of an Egyptian high **priest**. Joseph took an Egyptian name and when he died he was buried in the Egyptian manner.

Many of the details in the biblical story of Joseph can also be found in Egyptian sources. The Egyptians did believe that **dreams** could foretell the future and kings did employ dream interpreters. There is an Egyptian version of the story of the seven-year famine, set in the reign of King **Zoser**. Also, people of foreign birth did sometimes become high officials at the Egyptian court. Joseph may have lived in the **Second Intermediate Period**, when foreign kings were ruling the north of Egypt. We know that many people from Palestine settled in Egypt at this time, probably because of widespread famine. Some people have even identified Joseph with Yuya, the father-in-law of King **Amenhotep III**, but there is no real evidence of this.

Ka

The life force of a person or god (see **Afterlife**).

Karnak

The great temple complex of the god **Amun** at Karnak in northern **Thebes** was the biggest and most important in all Egypt. The first temple there was built by King Nebhepetra Mentuhotep in the **Middle Kingdom**, and for the next 2,000 years Egypt's rulers kept on adding to it. When they started to run out of space they just pulled down some of the old buildings and used the blocks to build new ones. By **Roman** times Karnak was a rambling complex of shrines, halls, **pylons**, statues and **obelisks** covering 3 square km (1.9 square miles). There were offices, workshops, schools and libraries, beautiful **gardens** with flower beds and **trees**, a lake and even a poultry yard for Amun's sacred geese.

In fact Karnak was not one complex but three – one for Amun, one for his wife Mut and one for Montu, the local war god. Inside Amun's complex were many other temples, including that of his son Khons. The Karnak temples were connected to Luxor temple, in southern Thebes, by roads lined with **sphinxes**. At **festival** times the statues of the **gods and goddesses** were carried in procession along these roads, cheered on their way by crowds lining the route. The main entrance to Karnak was connected to the Nile by a canal, and there was a quay where boats could tie up. Ordinary people could not go inside, but they were allowed to pray to special statues outside the walls.

Karnak was the richest temple complex in Egypt. It owned huge amounts of land both in Egypt and abroad, and employed thousands of people. In time its **priests** became very powerful and had great influence in the running of the country. During the **New Kingdom** King **Akhenaten** tried to take their power away by making Aten the national god instead of Amun, but after his death Karnak became more important than ever.

The Temple of Amun at Karnak.

*The god Khnum has the head of a long-horned ram. In this relief he also wears a wig and a **crown**.*

Khnum

Khnum was the god who shaped all living things on his potter's wheel. He was usually shown as a ram with long corkscrew horns, or as a ram-headed man. The ancient Egyptians' word for a ram is *ba*, which sounds like one of their words for the soul (see **Afterlife**). This is probably why Khnum was called the 'soul' of other gods, such as **Ra**. Khnum's temple on the island of Elephantine at **Aswan** is one of the oldest in **Egypt**.

Sacred rams were kept on the island and buried near the temple in stone **coffins**. This temple had a **Nilometer** to measure the height of the inundation (the annual flood) as it reached Egypt. The Egyptians believed that Khnum had power over the Nile. If he stopped the river from flooding, the fields wouldn't be irrigated and Egypt would starve (see **Zoser**).

A '**Festival** of the Potter's Wheel' was held at the temple of Esna to celebrate Khnum's creation of life. A hymn carved on the temple wall tells how Khnum formed gods, people, animals and plants and then brought them alive. It also describes how he made each part of the human body and invented all the languages of the world. Another hymn was sung to the god each morning. One verse goes: 'Wake up, fighting ram who chases his enemies and herds his followers. In peace, wake up, in peace!'

Khufu

Khufu was the ancient Egyptian king known to the **Greeks** as Cheops. He lived in the 24th century BC and reigned for about twenty-three years. A tiny ivory figurine is the only portrait of him that has survived. It was Khufu who built the Great Pyramid, one of the Seven Wonders of the Ancient World (see **Giza** and **Pyramids**). For nearly 4,500 years this was the tallest building on earth and it must have taken a large workforce many years of hard labour to complete it. None of Khufu's burial treasure survives, but two cedarwood **boats** were found in pits next to the Great Pyramid.

In Egyptian legend, Khufu was remembered as a cruel tyrant. A story written during the **Middle Kingdom** describes how he wanted to learn some of the secrets of the god **Thoth** to help him build his pyramid. The king summoned the cleverest magician in the land, an old peasant called Djedi. Khufu ordered Djedi to prove his power by bringing a man back to life after his head had been cut off. Djedi warned the king that human beings should never be treated in this way and revived **birds** and **animals** instead. Then the magician revealed that three **children** would soon be born to replace Khufu's family as rulers of **Egypt**. When the Greek historian Herodotus visited Egypt he was told that Khufu had reduced the whole country to misery. Khufu was accused of closing down the **temples** of the gods and forcing all his subjects to work on his pyramid.

Kings

Egypt was ruled by kings from about 3100 BC. Each king had far more power than anyone else in the **government**. The Egyptians knew that the body of the king was only human but they believed in an eternal spirit of kingship that was passed from ruler to ruler.

Each king was given a long string of **names** and titles that linked him to the gods. From the 4th **Dynasty** onwards most kings were called sons of **Ra**, the sun god. The king was closely identified with the falcon god **Horus** during his life and with **Osiris**, the god of the dead, when he died. Rulers such as **Hatshepsut** and **Amenhotep III** claimed to be children of the creator god **Amun**-Ra. From the **New Kingdom** onwards the term *per-aa*, which means 'great house' or palace, was often used for the king. The Greeks turned this Egyptian term into the word 'pharaoh'. Ever since then Egypt has been known as the 'Land of the Pharaohs'.

The Egyptians thought that a king's chief duty was to serve **Maat** (order and justice) and fight the forces of chaos. Kings did this in many different ways. The king was the head of government but he had a council to help him make

*An ivory carving of a king wearing the White **Crown** of Upper Egypt. This is one of the earliest known portraits of an Egyptian king.*

This tiny figurine is the only known portrait of Khufu.

decisions. The **viziers**, the governors of the provinces and all the other officials working for the state had to report to the king. The king was head of the legal system and people could appeal directly to him for justice. Every king was supposed to protect Egypt from foreign enemies and some rulers personally led the **army** into battle. Kings like **Thutmose III** and **Rameses II** spent long periods away from Egypt, fighting in the Near East. A prince or a queen was sometimes made co-ruler so that all these royal duties could be shared.

The king was also the religious head of state and had to take part in many religious ceremonies. In theory he was the high **priest** of every temple in the country and it is always the king who is shown making **offerings** to deities in paintings on temple walls. Only a king or queen could be shown touching a deity. One of the king's most important jobs was to keep the **gods and goddesses** happy by repairing their **temples** or building new ones. When a king died he had an elaborate **funeral** and **tomb** to make sure that his spirit joined the gods.

In Egyptian **art** most kings were shown as eternally young, strong, and handsome but we can see from the royal **mummies** that the reality was rather different. The office of kingship may have been beyond criticism but the people who held it weren't. Several ancient Egyptian folktales feature kings who were cruel, greedy or stupid. Some kings were murdered by relatives or high officials and nearly all the royal tombs were disturbed by robbers (see **Tomb robbers**). Even so, the system of rule by semi-divine kings lasted for about 3,000 years.

*A god (**Sobek**-Ra) offers the symbol of life to a king (**Amenhotep III**).*

Late Period (747–332 BC)

The Late Period (25th–30th **Dynasties**) was a time of turmoil in the Near East, during which **Egypt** suffered a whole series of invasions. It had been conquered by a king from **Nubia** at the end of the **Third Intermediate Period**. The Nubian kings who made up the 25th Dynasty had great respect for Egyptian religion. They repaired major **temples** and added new buildings and statues.

In the 7th century BC Egypt clashed with the most dangerous power in the Near East, a warlike people called the Assyrians (see **Egypt's neighbours**). After several attempts the Assyrians conquered Egypt and drove the 25th Dynasty back into Nubia. An Egyptian called Nekau who had collaborated with the Assyrians was left in charge of Egypt when the Assyrians had to withdraw most of their troops. Nekau was soon killed by Tanutamani, the last king of the 25th Dynasty, but then the Assyrians came back and defeated Tanutamani. As soon as the Assyrians turned their attention to fighting other enemies, Nekau's son Psamtek made Egypt independent again.

Psamtek I (Psammetichus) was the founder of the 26th Dynasty. The kings of this dynasty were buried in their native city of Sais, but their tombs have not been found. Psamtek I built a series of forts and hired **Greek** soldiers to help defend Egypt. **Art** and crafts flourished under the 26th Dynasty. Many beautiful objects were made in bronze and **faience**, while sculptors studied art from Egypt's glorious past and created new masterpieces.

By now the Assyrian empire had collapsed, but there was soon a new threat from the Persians (see **Egypt's neighbours**). The fourth king of the 26th Dynasty was defeated and killed by one of his own generals, a man named Amasis, who was noted for his coarse sense of humour. When Amasis became king, one of his **jokes** was to make his subjects worship a statue that had been made out of his footbath. Shortly after Amasis died Egypt was invaded by the Persians. Most of the royal family were killed and the body of Amasis was dug up and burned.

The kings of Persia were counted as the 27th Dynasty but there were many rebellions against them. A series of Egyptian leaders of the 28th to 30th Dynasties struggled for power. Egypt prospered briefly under the 30th Dynasty. King Nectanebo II was the last native Egyptian to rule ancient Egypt. In later legend he became a great magician, but his powers were not strong enough to save Egypt when the Persians invaded again. Nectanebo fled and Egypt once more became part of the Persian empire.

The Assyrian army attacks a town.

In the late 4th century BC, the Persian empire was taken over by Alexander the Great, the King of Macedonia. Alexander and the half-brother who succeeded him are shown as kings on the walls of Egyptian temples. After Alexander's death a Greek general called **Ptolemy** took control of Egypt. His family were to rule Egypt for 300 years (see **Graeco-Roman Period**).

*A Late Period statue of a **king** protected by the sacred ram of **Amun**.*

Law and order

The ancient Egyptians do not seem to have had a written set of laws and they certainly had no professional lawyers, so everyone probably spoke for themselves in court. Important cases were tried by a group of judges, who usually had other jobs as **priests** or administrators. The acting head of the legal system was the **vizier**, who was second-in-command to the king. Judges consulted the records of previous cases to help them come to a decision. Courts often met in the outer area of **temples**. Everyone had to swear an oath by their favourite god that they were telling the truth. Many people believed that the **gods** would strike them blind if they lied. The judges were allowed to have the accused beaten with sticks to make them confess. Sometimes witnesses were beaten too.

Each town or village seems to have had its own court. The judges were chosen from the most important and respected men living in the area. There was a police force, known as the Medjoy, but it mainly guarded state property. If a crime was committed the victim would complain to his or her local court and usually had to pay the **scribe** of the court to draw up a petition describing the crime. If the judges thought there was a case to answer they could order an investigation and question witnesses. These local courts often dealt with legal disputes about things like the

*The Abbott Papyrus records the confessions of a band of **tomb robbers** who were caught stealing from royal tombs in the **Valley of the Kings**.*

fair price for a young donkey, the ownership of a piece of land or the terms of a divorce settlement. Men and **women** seem to have been treated the same. Women could even bring cases against their husbands or fathers.

The law system started to change from the Ptolemaic period as **Greek** and **Roman** laws were introduced.

Letters

The earliest known Egyptian letters were written to a king nearly 4,500 years ago. Letters to or from the king were carried by government messengers. When ordinary people needed to send a letter they had to find a boat or a traveller going in the right direction. Most letters were about business matters but many Egyptians just wanted to keep in touch with family and friends while they were away from home.

Less than five per cent of the population could read or write, so people paid **scribes** to write their letters for them. When they received a letter themselves, they had to find someone who could read it aloud to them. This is why many

*A letter to an Egyptian king from a foreign ruler, found at **Amarna**.*

Egyptian letters sound like someone talking. 'How are you?' begins a 3,000-year-old letter. 'How are your family? I'm alive today, but tomorrow is in god's hands. I'm longing to see you and to hear about your daily doings. What's the point of my sending you all these letters, when you haven't sent one reply? What have I done to make you cross?'

Boys learning to be scribes had to copy out practice letters. It was polite to begin a letter by wishing long life and good health to the person you were writing to and promising to pray for him or her. **Papyrus** paper was expensive so short letters were sometimes written on **ostraca**, flakes of limestone or broken pieces of pottery. Royal letters to foreign rulers were inscribed on clay tablets. Archaeologists found 382 diplomatic letters dating to the 14th century BC in the city of **Amarna**. In the **Graeco-Roman Period** letters were often written on wooden boards. Thousands of letters in Greek and Latin have survived from this period, including love letters, wedding invitations and **tax** demands.

The most unusual letters to survive from ancient Egypt were those written to gods or to people who had died. Letters to the gods were delivered to **temples**. They usually asked a god for a favour and promised gifts in return. One man wrote to the god **Amun** asking him to grant a prayer in return for some date wine, foreign beer and white bread. Letters to the dead were posted in or near **tombs**. One grieving husband wrote to tell his dead wife that he was still missing her after three years.

Linen

Linen was easily the most popular fabric in Egypt, although wool from sheep and goats was also used to make warm cloaks and blankets for the winter. Linen, which was made from the stems of flax plants,

was an important export and its production was controlled by the **government**. Farmers harvested the flax at different stages: old plants had strong, tough fibres for making ropes and mats, while young plants provided the fine, soft fibres used to make cloth.

When the plants were ready they were pulled from the ground. Their stems were soaked and beaten to separate the fibres, which were then combed and rolled to prepare them for spinning. The art of spinning and weaving cloth was so old that the Egyptians believed their ancestors had learned it from the goddess **Isis** herself. Weaving was done by both men and women, but they used different types of loom. **Women** used the traditional flat ground loom and men used upright looms. When the cloth was finished it was inspected and graded by government officials. Patterned fabrics were sometimes woven from coloured thread, and linen was also embroidered or dyed with natural colours from plants. On the whole, though, the Egyptians preferred pure white cloth, bleached by the sun. **Clothes** were designed to use as little linen as possible because it was so precious. Old clothes were mended and worn-out garments re-used for things like washcloths and **mummy** wrappings.

Linen cloth.

Flax was harvested by pulling it up from the roots.

89

M

Maat

Maat was an ancient Egyptian word that meant truth, justice and order. The Egyptians believed that maat symbolized the way the world should be, with everything in perfect harmony. The opposite of maat was *isfet*, which meant chaos and evil. Maat was said to be the food and drink of the gods and every king of Egypt was supposed to fight for maat and against *isfet*.

Maat was also worshipped as a goddess, and judges wore an image of her as their badge of office. Maat was shown as a woman with an ostrich feather on her head and she sometimes had wings as well as arms or wore a feather-patterned dress. The goddess Maat was a daughter of the sun god **Ra** and one of her duties was to make him laugh. Figures of Maat were offered to the **gods** during **temple** services.

The judgement of the dead was said to take place in the 'Hall of the Double Maat'. The Egyptians believed that after death their hearts would be weighed against the feather of Maat. This would show how they had behaved when they were alive (see **Afterlife** and **Book of the Dead**).

A gold figure of Maat, probably once worn by a judge.

Magic

The ancient Egyptians believed in a magical power called *heka* which the gods used to create the world and protect it from the forces of chaos. Egyptian religion allowed people to use some forms of magic. Books of magic spells were kept in temple libraries and **priests** could specialize in magic. The Egyptians told stories about lector-priests who could read ancient books of magic and do wonderful things like turning a wax crocodile into a real one. Magic wands made in ivory or bronze were used to control supernatural forces. These wands were sometimes shaped like snakes, because the goddess of magic took the form of a snake.

Most ancient Egyptian magic was used to cure or protect people. **Doctors** not only prescribed drugs or carried out minor surgery, they also recited spells over their patients. These often told a story about a god who had been injured or was sick. In this way, the doctor summoned up supernatural forces that helped to heal the patient, just as they had once healed the god in the story. Doctors used magical statues of the god **Horus** to help cure scorpion or snake bites. They poured water over the statue so that it would absorb the power of the magical words and images carved on the statue, and then used this water to wash the wound.

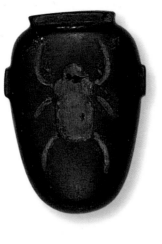

Heart-**scarabs** were thought to magically help the dead when they were being judged in the underworld.

The Egyptians thought that many illnesses or accidents were caused by ghosts, demons, angry deities or people with the evil eye, and that **children** were most at risk. This was one of the main reasons for wearing **amulets**. There were also protective spells that people could recite, such as those in 'The Book of Scaring Away an Enemy'. Many Egyptians seem to have been afraid that something would happen to them while they were asleep. There were spells to guard bedrooms, to drive away the scorpions, snakes and biting insects that came out at night, and to stop nightmares. Even the dead were thought to need magical help and were buried with written spells, amulets, funerary models and tomb paintings (see **Book of the Dead**).

In the **temples**, **priests** used magic to curse the enemies of the king and the state. Clay or wax figurines representing the leaders of foreign countries or Egyptian traitors were cursed, stabbed, burned and then buried. The Egyptians believed that the curses went on working in the **afterlife**, so this sort of punishment lasted forever.

Harmful forms of magic seem to have become more common by the **Graeco-Roman Period**. There were many nasty spells for sending people nightmares, making them go blind or forcing them to fall in love. The spells of this era are long and complex. Magicians had to find bizarre ingredients, such as blood from a tick feeding on a black dog or hair from a murdered man. They also had to do strange things, like rubbing their eyes with a mixture of falcon's eggs and myrrh, or painting magic symbols on the wings of a live bat. This kind of 'black magic' was banned by the church when Egypt became a Christian country.

The fearsome creatures on this ivory wand were summoned by magic to protect women and children.

Mastaba

The word 'mastaba' means 'bench' in Arabic. **Egyptologists** use it to describe a type of low, oblong tomb built over an underground burial chamber. The first mastabas were made for royalty, but by the **Old Kingdom**, when **kings** were buried in **pyramids**, other members of the court were allowed to build themselves mastabas in the royal **cemeteries**. Mastabas were built of mud-brick or stone. They looked a bit like houses and people thought of them as homes for the spirits of the dead. They had storerooms to hold all the things the dead person needed for the **afterlife**, and a chapel with a false door through which the spirit could come to receive **offerings**. The walls of these rooms were often decorated with paintings and carvings of the things the tomb-owner wanted to enjoy in the next world.

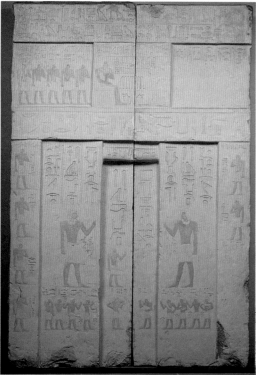

False doors allowed the dead person's spirit to go in and out of the tomb.

Mathematics

The **Greeks** are often credited with inventing mathematics. In fact the ancient Egyptians were using maths centuries before the Greeks. They knew how to calculate the area of a circle and the volume of a **pyramid**. The **hieroglyphic** script included seven signs for numbers of different values (see the box on page 93). Numbers were usually written with the smallest unit first and the largest unit last – the opposite to the modern system. Some fractions were written with parts of the damaged **Eye of Horus**, which were put back together by **Thoth**, the 'Reckoner of the Gods'.

Egyptian **children** learned mathematics by copying out standard

Old Kingdom mastaba at Giza. Tombs were called 'houses of eternity'.

problems and their answers. Some of these exercises survive, along with the teacher's corrections. We also have a few book-scrolls of more advanced arithmetic and geometry, which would have been consulted by people working in administration or on building projects. The Egyptians were mainly interested in mathematics for practical reasons. They wanted to work out things like the number of bricks needed to build a ramp of a certain size (see **Building**).

The challenge of building bigger and bigger pyramids forced the Egyptians to study geometry. The Rhind Mathematical Papyrus, which dates to around 1600 BC, works out problems about the volume of rectangles, triangles and pyramids. The last problem in this **papyrus** seems to be a joke. It is all about how much corn could be saved if 343 mice were eaten by forty-nine cats in seven houses.

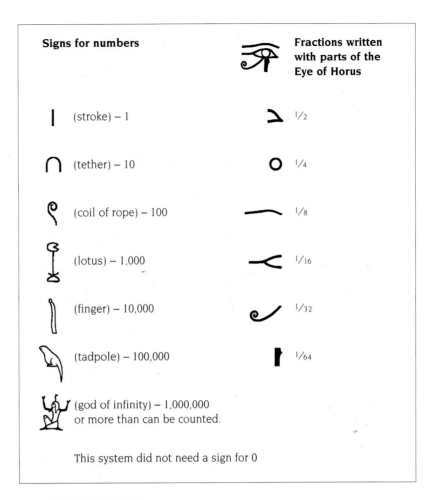

Signs for numbers		Fractions written with parts of the Eye of Horus	
|	(stroke) – 1	⌐	1/2
∩	(tether) – 10	○	1/4
ℓ	(coil of rope) – 100	—	1/8
ϒ	(lotus) – 1,000	⋎	1/16
|	(finger) – 10,000	⌐	1/32
⌐	(tadpole) – 100,000	▮	1/64
⚚	(god of infinity) – 1,000,000 or more than can be counted.		

This system did not need a sign for 0

*A page from the Rhind Mathematical Papyrus showing how to work out the volume of **pyramids**.*

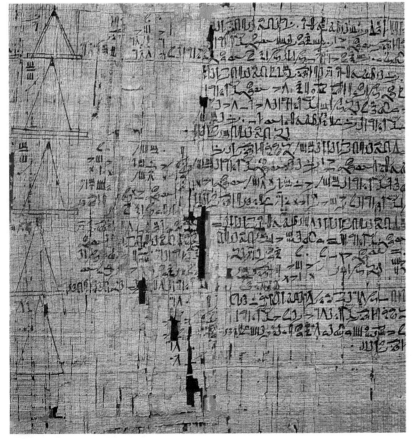

Medinet Habu

Medinet Habu, on the west bank of the Nile at **Thebes**, is the site of a huge temple built by King **Rameses III**. Next to the temple he had a little **palace** with its own bedroom, bathroom and toilet. This was joined to the temple by a balcony with a window at which the king would appear before his people at **festivals**.

Throne room in the palace of Rameses III at Medinet Habu.

Memphis

The ancient city of Memphis lay just south of Cairo, close to where the Nile Valley joins the Nile Delta. Memphis was Egypt's first capital. It is said to have been founded by King **Menes** in about 3100 BC.

Memphis.

Egyptian **Kings** always had a palace there and the **Old Kingdom** pharaohs were buried in **pyramids** in the **cemeteries** to the west of the city. Its most famous cemeteries are **Giza** and **Saqqara**.

Memphis is actually a **Greek** name. The city's Egyptian name – Men-nefer,

meaning 'established and beautiful' – was borrowed from one of the nearby royal pyramids. The city's chief deities were the creator god **Ptah** and his wife, the destroyer goddess **Sekhmet**. Ptah's temple was the most important building in the city. Close by was the house of the sacred **Apis bull**, which was worshipped as a form of the god **Osiris**.

Memphis remained Egypt's main port until the **Ptolemies** built **Alexandria** in the 4th century BC. Unfortunately, most of the city has since been destroyed and much of what remains lies buried underneath modern villages.

Menes

The name given by ancient historians to the first king of all Egypt (see **Early Dynastic Period**).

Metals

The mountains between the Nile and the Red Sea are rich in metal ores (stones containing metals – such as copper, lead, tin and **gold**). One of the first things the early Egyptians learned to do was to extract copper by heating copper ore in a fire until the metal within the stone melted and ran out. Copper was quite useful but rather soft, and after a while metalworkers learned to add a little tin to it to make bronze, which is much harder and better for tools and weapons (see **Warfare**). Gold, which was always precious, could easily be worked into **jewellery** and precious objects.

Metalworkers also used silver, which was even more valuable because it had to be imported. Sometimes gold and silver were mixed together to make an alloy called electrum.

Egyptian metalworkers were very skilful and could work metal either with or without heat. When melted over a fire, metals could be cast in clay or sand moulds to make objects of all sizes, from tiny beads and **amulets** to axeheads, swords and even massive temple doors. Lumps of cold metal could be hammered into flat sheets that could be made into vessels or used to cover wooden items such as **furniture**. Wire, made of thin strips cut from these sheets of metal, could be twisted or plaited into chains. Pieces of metal were joined together with molten metal (solder) or pins (rivets). Egyptian jewellers had many ways of decorating metal with engraved (chased) or raised (repoussé) designs, but one of their most beautiful techniques was to make a network of wires that was then filled with coloured stones or **glass**.

*This bronze statuette of the sacred **Apis bull** of Memphis was first modelled in wax, then cast in a mould. This method is called the lost wax technique.*

Bronze and copper vessels.

Middle Kingdom

(c.2055–1650 BC)

After the great age of the pyramid-builders (see **Old Kingdom**), **Egypt** split up again into several kingdoms (see **First Intermediate Period**). In the 21st century BC King Nebhepetra Mentuhotep defeated a rival dynasty and reunited Egypt. This was the start of the Middle Kingdom (11th–13th Dynasties). Mentuhotep built shrines for the local **gods and goddesses** all over Egypt as well as a splendid memorial temple at **Deir el-Bahri**. He was worshipped as a god in **Thebes** for 1,000 years after his death. The last king of Mentuhotep's line was succeeded by his **vizier** Amenemhet, who became the founder of the 12th Dynasty.

King Amenemhet built a new capital called Itjtawy ('Seizer of the Two Lands') near el-Lisht. The site of this royal city has never been found. The 12th Dynasty was not popular at first and Amenemhet was probably murdered. His son Senusret I (c.1965–1920 BC) made Egypt a great power again. An Egyptian poem describes Senusret I shooting enemies with his bow and calls him 'a fighter without equal'. The Egyptians conquered part of **Nubia** and defeated the Libyans (see **Egypt's neighbours**). King **Senusret III** (1874–1855 BC) was a stern king who built a chain of forts to subdue all of Nubia and also reduced the power of families who governed the provinces of Egypt. His son King Amenemhet III was a great builder. His huge funerary temple at Hawara was one of the most famous buildings in the ancient world.

The 12th Dynasty ended with the reign of Queen Sobekneferu. It was unusual for a woman to rule Egypt, but there were probably no princes in the royal family at that time. The **kings** of the 13th Dynasty continued to rule from Itjtawy, but they gradually became less powerful. The Middle Kingdom came to an end when rival **dynasties** of kings took over part of the Delta (see **Second Intermediate Period**).

The Middle Kingdom royal **pyramids** have weathered badly and few Middle Kingdom **temples** or palaces remain. They were mostly pulled down and

*Part of a wooden **coffin** made during the Middle Kingdom. The fine detail of the painted **hieroglyphs** and symbols is typical of this period.*

Statue of an official who lived during the Middle Kingdom.

replaced by bigger buildings during the **New Kingdom**. The **art** of the Middle Kingdom was of very high quality. The portrait sculpture and royal **jewellery** of the 12th Dynasty were outstanding and beautiful paintings survive on some Middle Kingdom **coffins** and tomb walls. The Middle Kingdom was also a golden age of Egyptian literature. In later times Egyptian **children** learned to write by copying **stories**, poems and books of **wisdom** written in the Middle Kingdom.

Min

Min is one of the oldest known gods. He usually wore a headdress with two tall feathers and a long ribbon and carried a flail, a kind of whip used to drive animals. Min was in charge of making Egypt fertile. He made the crops grow and helped animals and people to have large families. Images of Min were carried round the fields at harvest time.

Moses

The story of Moses is told in the Book of Exodus in the Bible. Many Hebrews settled in **Egypt** during the time of **Joseph**, and the Egyptians later forced the Hebrew people into slavery and killed their male children. Moses was found floating on the river in an ark made of rushes and an Egyptian princess adopted him. This is rather similar to the myth of the god **Horus**, who was born on a floating island in the marshes and fostered by a royal goddess.

Moses grew up in the palace of Pharaoh, the king of Egypt. He fled the country after killing a cruel Egyptian overseer and had a vision of God in a burning bush. He then returned to Egypt to rescue the Hebrews and lead them to the Promised Land. Moses and his brother Aaron went to the palace and showed

Pharaoh that they were more powerful than his court magicians. Pharaoh refused to let the Hebrews go, so Moses called down the Seven Plagues, which included frogs, lice, flies, locusts and hail, and diseases that killed all the domestic animals and the first-born son in every Egyptian family. The Hebrews escaped but Pharaoh came after them with an army, so Moses asked God to part the waters of the Red Sea. The Hebrews crossed safely but the Egyptians were drowned. Moses and his people then began their long journey through the Sinai desert.

No part of this story is found in ancient Egyptian sources. Moses is probably a short version of a common Egyptian name such as Ramose or Thutmose. Childless Egyptians sometimes adopted **slaves** or the children of slaves, so the story of Moses' adoption by a princess would not be unusual. It is possible that he lived in the 14th century BC, since his message that there was only one God has been compared with the ideas of the 'Heretic Pharaoh' **Akhenaten**.

It is more likely, however, that Moses was born in the 13th century BC, when **Rameses II** was building a new capital city in the Delta. It was the custom in Egypt to conscript people to work on state **building** projects and no exceptions would have been made for foreign settlers. There is no evidence that any Egyptian king was drowned, but Rameses certainly did lose his first-born son. The sea that parted for Moses may have been one of the tidal lakes of the eastern Delta rather than the Red Sea. For centuries pilgrims have tried to follow the route of Moses through Sinai, which is now part of modern Egypt. A shrub growing in the garden of St Catherine's monastery on the slopes of Mount Sinai is said to be the original burning bush from which God spoke to Moses.

Mummies

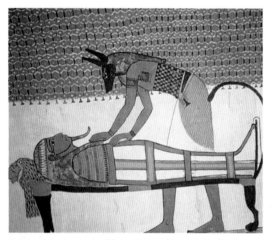

A mummy is a dead body that has been preserved by drying. Mummification sometimes happens naturally when bodies are buried in dry places, but many peoples around the world, including the ancient Egyptians, developed artificial techniques for preserving their dead in this way. The first Egyptian mummies were probably produced by accident when bodies buried in the desert were dried out by the hot sand. Their lifelike appearance, with bones, sinews, skin, hair, teeth and nails all intact, may have made the early Egyptians wonder about life after death.

They decided that the dead needed their bodies for the **afterlife** and tried to find ways to preserve them. Their first

*Painting from the tomb of Sennedjem at **Deir el-Medina**. Embalming priests sometimes wore jackal masks when acting out the part of the god Anubis.*

attempts were unsuccessful: burying the bodies in wooden **coffins** or brick **tombs** prevented the sand from drying them out, and although wrapping them in bandages held the bodies together, it did not prevent them from rotting. But by the **Old Kingdom**, embalmers had discovered how a kind of salt called **natron** could be used to dry and preserve bodies.

The process took seventy days and was carried out in special tents in the desert, far away from where people lived.

First the body was washed, then the brain, which was not thought to be important, was pulled out through the nose with an iron hook and thrown away. Next, the lungs, liver, stomach and intestines were taken out through a slit cut in the left side of the body, then embalmed and placed in **canopic jars**.

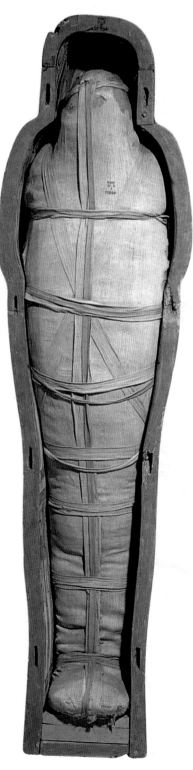

Mummy of a priestess from Thebes. After a mummy had been wrapped, it was placed inside a coffin made of wood or cartonnage. Sometimes these coffins were brightly painted with pictures of gods and with prayers to protect the dead person.

The heart was kept with the body because people believed the dead person would need it in order to be judged in the afterlife. Then the embalmers cleaned out the body and covered it with natron, which dried it out and killed the bacteria that cause decay. After forty days the body was cleaned again and stuffed with **linen** or sawdust, together with **perfumes** and sweet-smelling herbs. The skin was rubbed with ointment to make it supple, then coated in melted resin, which made it strong and waterproof. Our word 'mummy' comes from *mummiya*, the Arabic name for bitumen. Next came the bandaging with strips of linen. **Amulets** to protect the dead person were often put into the wrappings, and finally a mask was placed over the head and shoulders (see **Cartonnage**).

Birds, fish and animals were mummified as well as humans. People often had their favourite **pets** embalmed, and **sacred animals** such as the **Apis bull** were mummified and given special burials. In **Graeco-Roman** times, pilgrims visiting temples could buy animal mummies to dedicate as **offerings** in special catacombs. Some of these animal **cemeteries** contain millions of mummies.

Mummies of the Roman period were often bandaged in a very elaborate way. Instead of a mask, they sometimes had a portrait of the dead person.

The body of this predynastic farmer, who lived around 3500 BC, was preserved by burial in the hot desert sand.

The jackal was the sacred animal of the god Anubis. Pilgrims to religious centres like Memphis could buy mummified jackals to offer as gifts to Anubis.

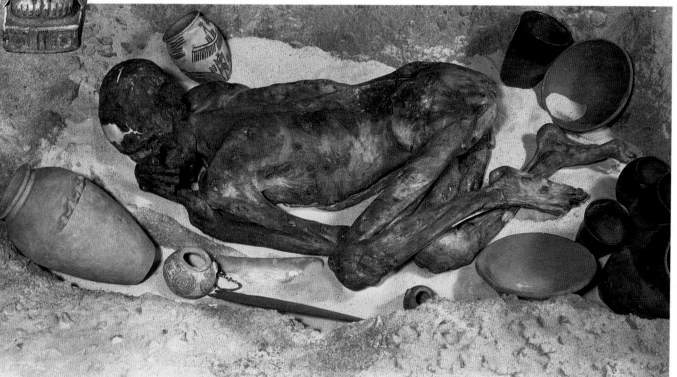

Female musicians. Two of the girls keep time by clapping, while another sings a song, accompanied on the double flute by the fourth girl.

Music

In some ways Egyptian love songs were exactly like the pop songs of today. Everybody knew the latest songs and wanted to hear them at parties. Quite often the words were about people becoming lovesick:

**I yearn for your love day and night,
I lie awake long hours, until dawn!
Your shape revives my heart,
All my desire is for you!**

Although we know a lot about ancient Egyptian musical instruments, we know hardly anything about the music played on them because the Egyptians never wrote their music down. However, we do know about the songs they sang, because the words were often set down on **papyrus** or on **tombs** and temple walls. The words of these songs tell us that guests at feasts liked to hear romantic love songs, and that farmers sang to their oxen to encourage them to work harder!

Clapping rhythms were an important accompaniment to song and **dance** performances, while flutes, harps and lutes provided the music. Some performers used clappers, castanets, tambourines and rattles to keep time. Both sexes could be musicians. Some instruments were played only by men or only by women, especially in temples, where music accompanied the hymns sung to **gods and goddesses**. **Priestesses** in temple rituals used a special kind of rattle called a sistrum, which was associated with the goddess **Hathor**. Hathor herself was connected with music. Carvings on her temples often show **priests** playing musical instruments, and her son Ihy was the god of music. Another deity associated with music was the god **Bes**, who is often shown singing and dancing.

Wooden model of a female harpist.

This carved bowl shows a procession of temple dancers and musicians. Their instruments include pipes, clappers, a drum and a stringed instrument called a lyre.

Names

The ancient Egyptians used only personal names, not surnames. Children were named on the seventh day after they were born. The personal name chosen for the baby was followed by words identifying it as the child of its parents. If only one parent's name was included – as in 'Ahmose, son of Ebana' – it was often the mother's. Egyptian personal names usually had a particular meaning. Some were whole sentences like Radjedefankhef ('**Ra** has said that he will live'). Others referred to a deity, as in Hornakht ('**Horus** is strong'), or to a religious **festival**, as in Mutemwiya ('Mut is in her festival boat'). Boys were sometimes named after the reigning king, while girls' names often included words such as *nedjem* (sweet) or *nefer* (beautiful). Some names, such as Ahmose, were used by both males and females. If a name was long and complicated, a shorter version was usually used. Someone called Rameses might be called Mesy, and nicknames like Panehsi (the Nubian) or Sheri (little one) were also common. Legal documents gave the name by which a person was normally called as well as his or her 'official' name.

Egyptian **kings** had more names than anyone else. The two main ones were the throne or coronation name (the prenomen) and the family name (the nomen). A king did not take a throne name until the start of his reign. (In this book kings' family names are used.) From around the 26th century BC the king's two main names were written in **cartouches**. Most kings had three more names – the Horus name, the **Two Ladies** name and the Horus of Gold name – so writing the full title of a king took up a lot of space.

The Egyptians thought names were vital to people's identity. They hoped that inscribed **tombs** and statues would make their names live on after death. They believed that as long as a dead person's name was still being spoken, his or her spirit would survive. Criminals could be punished by having their name replaced by an insulting one such as 'Ra hates him'. In some tombs the name of the owner has been hammered out by someone trying to hurt that person after death. In the **afterlife** the spirits of the dead had to memorize the names of the demons they would meet, because knowing a being's true name gave you power over them.

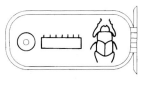

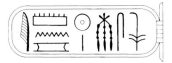

The throne and family names of three famous kings.

Thutmose III
(top two cartouches)

Rameses II
(middle two cartouches)

Tutankhamun
(bottom two cartouches).

Natron

A natural salt made up of sodium carbonate (washing soda) and sodium bicarbonate (baking soda). It was used both to make **glass** and in the process of mummification (see **Mummies**).

Nefertari

Nefertari was the favourite wife of the great pharaoh **Rameses II** (c.1279–1213 BC). She was constantly shown by his side until her death in the twenty-fourth year of his reign. When Rameses built his huge rock-cut temple at **Abu Simbel** he had a matching smaller temple cut for Nefertari. Inside, she is shown being crowned by two goddesses. An inscription states that Rameses made this temple for Nefertari 'for whose sake the sun shines'. None of Rameses' other wives was ever honoured in this way.

Rameses and Nefertari had seven or eight children, but apparently the sons all died before their father. In Year 21 of Rameses' reign Nefertari wrote to the Queen of the Hittites (see **New Kingdom**): 'With me, your sister, all goes well. With my country all goes well.' When Nefertari died, Rameses had a beautiful tomb made for her in the **Valley of the Queens**. The walls are covered with wonderful paintings of Nefertari being welcomed to the **afterlife** by **gods and goddesses**. In recent times salt got into the walls and damaged the paintings, but the tomb has now been restored.

*Statues of Queen Nefertari and her husband, **Rameses II**, on the front of the 'Small Temple' at **Abu Simbel**.*

Nefertiti

Nefertiti was the chief wife of King **Akhenaten** (c.1352–1336 BC). Her name means 'A Beautiful One Has Come'. It has been suggested that she was a foreign princess, but it is more likely that she was Akhenaten's cousin. Nefertiti seems to have had great influence over her husband.

The famous head of Queen Nefertiti found in a sculptor's workshop at Amarna. The crown she is wearing is unique to Nefertiti.

She was shown on the walls of his first temple making **offerings** to the sun god Aten, and colossal statues of her stood in the temple courtyard. All this was unusual for an Egyptian queen. Nefertiti also wore a unique crown.

Akhenaten and Nefertiti had six daughters. Carvings from their capital city of **Amarna** show charming images of the royal family. In a typical scene, the little princesses have clambered onto their parents' laps and one of them is playing with Nefertiti's earrings. No Egyptian king or queen had ever been shown in such an informal way before. However, the family life of Akhenaten and Nefertiti may not really have been as happy as it looked. Akhenaten married at least two of his daughters and had children by them. Nefertiti was no longer mentioned by the 14th year of Akhenaten's reign, when he took a co-ruler called Smenkhara. Akhenaten is shown kissing Smenkhara, so this 'king' might have been Nefertiti under a new name, although he could alternatively have been Akhenaten's son or his half-brother. The date of Nefertiti's death is uncertain but she seems to have been buried in the royal tomb at Amarna. Only a few fragments of her burial goods survive.

In 1912 a team of German archaeologists excavated a sculptor's workshop at Amarna, where they found a painted head of Queen Nefertiti, which quickly became one of the most famous sculptures in the world. A local official allowed the Germans to take this treasure back to Berlin. The head, which is still in Berlin, shows that Nefertiti was one of the most beautiful women who ever lived.

Neith

Neith was a goddess who was both loved and feared. She was linked with war and **hunting**, but in some myths she was the creator of the world and one of her titles was 'the mother and father of all things'. Neith was said to have made both order and chaos, good and evil. She was usually shown as a mature woman wearing the Red Crown of Lower Egypt (see **Crowns**). She had a mysterious symbol, which could be a shield crossed with arrows or some kind of beetle.

Neith was very important in the **Early Dynastic Period** when queens had names like Merneith ('Loved by Neith'). She was one of the four goddesses who watched over the dead and was often shown on the east side of royal **coffins**. Her blessing was asked for on shrouds and **mummy** bandages. As a marsh goddess she was the 'nurse of crocodiles' and the mother of **Sobek**, the crocodile god. Neith was the local goddess of a place called Sais in the Delta. The ancient Greek writer Herodotus tells us that her temple at Sais was a great **stone** building with a sacred lake and many huge statues. The **Greeks** thought that she was very like their goddess Athena.

A bronze figure of the goddess Neith.

Nekhbet

A southern Egyptian vulture goddess (see **Two Ladies**).

Nephthys

*This painted wooden statuette shows Nephthys mourning her brother **Osiris**.*

The goddess Nephthys was one of the children of the earth god and the sky goddess (see **Creation myths**). She was always overshadowed by her sister **Isis**. Nephthys means 'Lady of the Mansion' and the **hieroglyphs** for her name usually form her headdress. She could be shown as a woman or as a kite (a small bird of prey). In Egyptian myth Isis was happily married to their good brother **Osiris**, while Nephthys was forced to marry their evil brother **Seth**. In some versions of the story Nephthys is also married to Osiris, and the jackal god **Anubis** is their son. Nephthys was a loyal sister to Isis. After Seth murdered Osiris, she helped her sister to find the body and bring it back to life. The two goddesses were often shown weeping for Osiris – Nephthys standing or kneeling at the head of the body and Isis at the foot.

Nephthys had no **temples** of her own, but she was an important figure in burial **art** because she was one of the four goddesses who protected the bodies of the dead. She is shown on the north side of **coffins** and on chests holding **canopic jars**. The bandages used to wrap **mummies** were sometimes called 'the hair of Nephthys' and beautiful **women** were chosen to play the roles of the two sisters at **funerals**. They kept watch over the mummy and then walked beside the coffin to the **tomb**. They also sang laments for Osiris and the words of some of these songs survive. One verse goes: 'I am Nephthys, your beloved sister! Your enemy is beaten, he does not exist, I am with you as your protector for all eternity.'

New Kingdom
(c.1550–1069 BC)

Egypt was at the height of its power and influence during the New Kingdom (18th–20th **Dynasties**). There are many historical records for the New Kingdom, including **letters** to and from **kings**, and detailed accounts of battles (see **Warfare**). The excavation of towns such as **Amarna** and **Deir el-Medina** has revealed a lot about daily life in this period. The **art** and **architecture** of the 18th Dynasty was a high point of Egyptian culture.

By the end of the **Second Intermediate Period**, the kings of the 17th Dynasty had broken the power of the Hyksos invaders (see **Egypt's neighbours**). Ahmose, the first ruler of the 18th Dynasty, finished the task of driving the Hyksos leaders out of Egypt, then followed them into Palestine and Syria and conquered territories there. After he had made the northern border of Egypt secure, Ahmose led his army south into **Nubia**. He reorganized the **government** of Egypt and rewarded his soldiers with gifts of land and **slaves**. Ahmose's reign was seen as the start of a new era for Egypt.

The next two kings, Amenhotep I and Thutmose I, led their armies in person and won further victories. Most of Nubia and parts of Syria and Palestine now came under Egyptian control. Thutmose I was probably the first ruler to be buried in the **Valley of the Kings**. There were fewer military campaigns under Thutmose II and Queen **Hatshepsut**. During Hatshepsut's reign a trading expedition was sent to Punt in Africa, which was further south than any Egyptian had ever travelled before (see **Trade**). Hatshepsut's nephew, **Thutmose III** (c.1479–1425 BC), was Egypt's most successful warrior king. He led his **army** and navy on seventeen campaigns. The cities and states that he conquered were forced to pay tribute (gifts) to Egypt in return for 'protection'.

The constant flow of tribute in the form of **animals**, slaves and foreign goods, and the **gold** in the neighbouring deserts made Egypt very wealthy. Thutmose and his successors used much of this wealth to build **temples** and replace small mud-brick buildings with large **stone** ones. The **priests** who ran the major temples, such as **Karnak**, became very powerful. In the 14th century BC King **Akhenaten** tried to end this power by closing down many temples and promoting the worship of one god. He built a new capital at Amarna and took little interest in Egypt's empire. His successors soon reversed his policies. The 18th Dynasty ended with Horemheb, another soldier king.

The kings of the 19th Dynasty were descended from a **vizier** called Rameses. King Sety I succeeded in protecting most of Egypt's empire from a warrior race known as the Hittites (see **Egypt's neighbours**). His son, **Rameses II** (c.1279–1213 BC), fought several campaigns against the Hittites before deciding to make peace with them. He spent the rest of his very long reign on a massive **building** campaign. Everything had to be bigger and better under Rameses II. He built a new capital in the Delta and many temples in Egypt and Nubia, including the rock-cut temples of **Abu Simbel**.

An **ushabti** of King Ahmose, the first great ruler of the New Kingdom.

32191.

King **Rameses III** celebrates his victory over the foreigners who tried to invade Egypt. In this scene **scribes** are recording the number of enemies killed in the battle.

In the 12th century BC the kings of the 20th Dynasty faced many problems. Egypt was attacked by the Libyans and by the Sea Peoples (see **Egypt's neighbours**). **Rameses III**, the last great ruler of the New Kingdom, defeated these invaders but most of the empire was lost. Egypt became poorer, and the government more corrupt. By the end of the 12th century economic problems had led to a breakdown in **law and order**. In **Thebes** royal tombs were robbed (see **Tomb robbers**) and temples were raided by bands of Libyans. The kings of the 20th Dynasty still controlled the north. In the south of the country, the real power was in the hands of generals and high priests (see **Third Intermediate Period**). The New Kingdom officially ended with Rameses XI (c.1099–1069 BC), the last king to have a tomb cut in the Valley of the Kings.

Nile

The main river of **Egypt**.

Nilometer

The annual Nile flood was the most important event in the ancient Egyptian **year**, and its height was crucial. If it was too low, there would not be enough water to grow **food**, but if it was too high, fields and dams would be washed away. As soon as the water began to rise each summer, officials started to keep a check on its height using Nilometers –

Nilometer on Elephantine Island at **Aswan**.

huge stone staircases going down into the river. They watched how long it took for the water to cover the steps in order to work out how fast the flood was rising and how high it was likely to get.

Nubia

The land of Nubia, to the south of **Egypt**, played an important role in Egyptian history. The Egyptians thought of Nubia as a foreign land and dreaded its hot deserts, but they were always trying to control it because it was the main source of their **gold** and a major **trade** route for precious African goods such as ebony, ivory and incense. The strong, tough Nubians were also in great demand in Egypt as soldiers and policemen.

Egyptians were trading and mining in Nubia as early as the **Old Kingdom**, and the **Middle Kingdom** pharaoh **Senusret III** built a chain of forts there to act as bases for these activities. He set up a **stela** in one of them, describing his ruthless conquest of Nubia: 'I have plundered their women and carried off their underlings, gone to their wells, driven off their bulls, torn up their corn and set fire to it ...'

During the **Second Intermediate Period**, a powerful Nubian dynasty was able to push the Egyptians out of their land, but they were back during the **New Kingdom**, occupying the whole northern part of the country. Kings such as **Rameses II** built enormous **temples** such as **Abu Simbel** as symbols of their power in Nubia and as a warning against rebellion.

Although the power struggle between Egypt and Nubia (known to the Egyptians as 'Kush') continued over the

The Nubian prince Heqanefer visiting the court of King **Tutankhamun**.

The Nubian pharaoh Taharqo ruled Egypt from 690 BC to 664 BC. Here he is shown as a **sphinx**.

centuries, the two countries had a lot in common. Later Nubian kings were buried in **pyramids**, built temples to Egyptian gods such as **Amun**, used Egyptian **hieroglyphs** and had themselves shown as **sphinxes**. In the **Third Intermediate Period** the powerful Nubian kingdom of Napata actually took control of Egypt. Its kings ruled as the 25th Dynasty until they were pushed back into Nubia by Assyrian invaders (see **Egypt's neighbours**).

After this time Egypt and Nubia remained separate, although there was another powerful Nubian kingdom at Meroë during the **Graeco-Roman Period**, and Egypt's Greek and Roman rulers built temples to Egyptian and Nubian gods at northern Nubian sites like Dendur. The Dendur temple is now in New York, presented by Egypt as a token of gratitude for the United States' contribution to saving the Nubian monuments threatened with flooding after the High Dam at **Aswan** was built.

Nut

Many religions had a god of the sky but the Egyptians had a sky goddess. Nut was the daughter of the air god and the sister of the earth god (see **Creation myths**). She was the mother of four important deities: **Osiris**, **Isis**, **Nephthys** and **Seth**. As the sky goddess Nut was shown either as a nude woman arched above the earth or as a giant cow with starry markings. Huge figures of her are found on the ceilings of **temples** and royal **tombs**. She was said to swallow the sun every evening and give birth to it again every morning (see **Underworld Books**), so she was known as 'the sow who eats her own piglets'. Sow-shaped **amulets** of Nut were popular in **Roman** Egypt.

One of Nut's symbols was a water jar and the sycamore was her sacred **tree**. Tomb paintings show her leaning out of a sycamore tree to offer bread and water to the souls of the newly dead. Nut also protected the dead in their **coffins** and helped them to be born again. One spell written inside **pyramids** says: 'Oh my mother Nut, spread yourself above me so that I can be placed among the unchanging stars and never die.'

*The sky goddess Nut painted on the inside of a **coffin** lid.*

Oasis

An oasis is a place in the desert where underground water comes to the surface, making it possible for people to live and grow food there. Most of the oases in **Egypt** are in the desert west of the Nile. The five most important ones are called Kharga, Dakhla, Farafra, Bahariya and **Siwa**. In ancient times they were important as stopping places for traders crossing the desert, and were famous for their dates and grapes. People who disagreed with the **government** were sometimes sent to live in the oases, where they could not cause so much trouble. The largest oases were like country towns, with public buildings, **temples** and **cemeteries**.

Siwa oasis.

Obelisk

An obelisk is a tall, thin **stone** pillar with four tapering sides and a little **pyramid** (called a 'pyramidion') on top. Obelisks were put up in front of **temples** and **tombs**. Their tips were sometimes covered in **gold** to reflect the sunlight. **Kings** and **queens** liked to set up obelisks carved with their **names** to make themselves famous.

Obelisks were usually made from a single piece of stone. If one broke when it was being cut from the rock it was left there and the stonecutters started again

The obelisk of Thutmose I at ***Karnak***.

somewhere else. The roughly-cut obelisks were taken to their destination on special barges pulled by lots of small boats. Nobody is sure how they were set up, but the workmen probably used ropes and wooden rollers to pull them into place (see **Building**).

Egypt's **Roman** rulers liked to collect obelisks and statues to decorate their cities, which is why there are now more obelisks in Rome than any other place in the world. Egyptian obelisks became very fashionable in the rest of the world during the 18th and 19th centuries. European architects and gardeners included obelisks in their designs, and collectors started bringing back genuine ancient obelisks from **Egypt**. Two of the most famous are the 'Cleopatra's Needle' obelisks now on the Thames Embankment in London and in Central Park, New York. Both of these were first set up by **Thutmose III** at **Heliopolis**. They were taken to **Alexandria** in Roman times and then to their new homes in 1878 and 1880 respectively.

Offerings

The ancient Egyptians offered gifts to higher powers in the hope of getting something in return. These offerings could be natural produce such as fruit, vegetables and meat, or man-made items such as textiles or bottles of **perfume**. The most common scene in ancient Egyptian **art** showed people making offerings to **gods** or to the dead.

Because food was essential in life, the Egyptians thought that the *ka* (spirit) of a dead person would still need to be fed in the **afterlife**. Scenes of people who had died sitting in front of a table of food offerings were shown on tomb walls and **stelae**. In these scenes a whole meal – including cuts of meat, loaves of bread, and fruit and vegetables – is usually piled onto the table. Wealthy people arranged for regular supplies of food to be brought to their tomb 'to nourish their *ka*'. If these supplies failed, the dead could magically feed from the offerings pictured on their

A copper offering set from a ***tomb***.

*This figure is one of a series showing the agricultural produce of all the districts of **Egypt**. The Egyptians believed that a share of everything the land produced should be offered to the gods.*

tomb walls or on the offering table (see **Food and drink**). Tomb stelae are usually inscribed with an 'offering formula'. This promises the dead person plenty of bread, beer, clothing, and oils for the skin. Reading an offering text aloud to help a dead person was a very pious thing to do.

Statues of the gods also needed offerings of 'every good thing on which a god lives'. They were treated like important people and given food, **clothes**, **jewellery**, **cosmetics** and scented oils every day. Animal sacrifices were an important part of Egyptian religion. Large **temples** had their own slaughter-yards where **priests** inspected the **animals** to make sure they were healthy. Only the best quality meat could be offered to deities.

When ordinary people visited a temple they brought water or beer for the deity. If they could afford it, they burned incense, presented **flowers**, or roasted a duck to give to the god. One Egyptian text says that a god 'prefers the loaf of the good man to the ox of the wicked man'. Figurines, plaques and jewellery were also offered by people who had special prayers to say. When the shrines got too full, these gifts were buried in pits in the temple grounds. Thousands of temple offerings have survived to the present day because of this custom.

Old Kingdom
(*c*.2686–2181 BC)

In later times people thought of the Old Kingdom (3rd–6th **Dynasties**) as Egypt's 'Golden Age'. The country was firmly united under a very efficient **government**. The king had a great army of civil servants to carry out his orders and Egypt was powerful enough to bully its neighbours. Many expeditions went out to exploit the mineral wealth of the deserts and to **trade** with other nations. New statues were made for the **temples** of the **gods**. These temples were quite small and were mainly built of mud-brick. The **kings** of Egypt were honoured as living gods and their monuments were made of **stone**.

The Old Kingdom was the great era of **pyramid** building. King **Zoser** was buried under a large step pyramid during the 3rd Dynasty. Several kings of the 4th Dynasty built huge straight-sided pyramids at Meidum, Dashur and **Giza**. Each royal pyramid had two temples joined by a causeway. This whole group of buildings is known as a pyramid complex. Small towns were built on the edge of the desert to house the **priests** who served in the pyramid temples. Some of the finest statues ever carved were made to adorn these pyramid complexes. To produce so much **art** and **architecture** in such a short time was a great feat of organization. King **Khufu**, the builder of the Great Pyramid, was remembered in Egyptian legend as a cruel tyrant. His vast pyramid may have cost the country too much in **taxes** and labour. Never again did Egyptian kings build such gigantic monuments.

At the end of the 4th Dynasty there was some kind of power struggle and a new line of kings took the throne. The rulers of the 5th Dynasty called themselves 'Sons of **Ra**'. They built stone temples for Ra, the sun god. The early 5th Dynasty pyramid complexes at Abusir are

A view of the Old Kingdom royal cemetery at **Giza**.

smaller than the 4th Dynasty ones but they were decorated with many fine reliefs. During the late 5th and the 6th Dynasties kings and **queens** built their pyramids in the ancient royal cemetery at **Saqqara**. These pyramids were inscribed with the Pyramid Texts, which were meant to help the dead king to reach his place in heaven.

The officials who helped to run the country also had splendid **tombs** (see **Mastaba**) and funerary statues. Painted reliefs on the tomb walls show scenes from people's careers and depict the ideal world they hoped to inhabit in the **afterlife**. Far from being gloomy, these tombs reflect the joy of life. Egyptian art reached a high point during the late Old Kingdom, but the country itself was already in decline. The climate was getting drier and this may have led to famines. The central government gradually

Wooden statue from an Old Kingdom tomb.

lost power to the nomarchs who ruled the provinces (see **Egypt**). King Pepy II came to the throne in about 2278 BC and seems to have reigned for ninety-four years. By the end of this incredibly long reign the king must have been far too old and weak to control Egypt. The 6th Dynasty seems to have finished with a Queen Nitiqret and Egypt began to break up (see **First Intermediate Period**).

Opening of the Mouth

A rite to give life to a **mummy** or a statue (see **Funerals**).

Oracles

An oracle is a supernatural power that can answer questions about the past, the present or the future. Statues of Egyptian **gods** were consulted as oracles from the 2nd millennium BC. Oracles in other countries were famous for giving answers that were difficult to understand, but in **Egypt** the god's answer was usually a plain yes or no. During **festivals**, groups

A boat-shrine carried by **priests**.

of **priests** carried small statues of the gods out of the **temples** in boat-shaped shrines. When the god was asked a question the boat-shrine would move forward for yes or backward for no. Ordinary people asked questions such as 'Will I get better?' or 'Will I be promoted?'. At the great temple of **Karnak**, the god **Amun** was asked to approve the decisions of **kings** and high priests. If the boat-shrine of the god stopped in front of someone during a procession at Karnak, that person was marked out as special. **Thutmose III** claimed that this had happened to him when he was a boy. It was taken as a sign that Amun had chosen Thutmose to be the next king.

Legal disputes (see **Law and order**) were sometimes decided by an oracle rather than by a human court, because the gods were thought to know the truth about what had happened in the past and the secrets of people's hearts. The oracle might have been asked to declare who was the true owner of a piece of land or who was hiding stolen goods. It would do this by choosing from a list of names that were read aloud. People did not always accept the verdict straight away, however. One man accused of theft was found guilty by three oracles before he broke down and confessed.

In later times the most famous oracle was in a temple of Amun at the **oasis** of **Siwa**. Travellers of many races made the difficult journey across the desert to ask this oracle questions. In the **Graeco-**

Roman Period priests made statues of the gods speak by whispering into a metal tube hidden in the base of the statue.

Osiris

Osiris was the god who gave the ancient Egyptians hope of a life after death. He was the oldest son of the earth god Geb and the sky goddess **Nut** (see **Creation myths**). Osiris was the first king of **Egypt**. His reign was a golden age during which he taught humans how to farm the land and make all the things they needed. But he was murdered by his jealous brother **Seth**. In some versions of the story Osiris was drowned in the **Nile**. The Egyptians thought of this crime as the worst thing that had ever happened. The god **Anubis** turned the body of Osiris into the first **mummy**. His loving wife **Isis** brought up their son **Horus** to avenge his father's death. Osiris could not return to the land of the living but he did rise again to become king of the dead.

Osiris was usually shown as a mummy wearing a headdress with horns and feathers known as an *atef*-crown (see **Crowns**). He often held the crook and flail, which were symbols of royalty. His skin was painted black like the rich soil of Egypt, or green like the new growth of plants. The most important **temples** of Osiris were at a place called **Abydos**.

At first Osiris seems to have been a grim god who ruled over a dark underworld where the souls of the dead could be horribly punished. Even the other **gods** were afraid of the demons who served Osiris. However, he was later seen as gentle and merciful. The dead were judged in his presence and those who had lived good lives became shining spirits in his court (see **Afterlife**). It was polite to refer to any dead person as 'an Osiris'. Everyone hoped they would rise from the dead like Osiris and enjoy a new life in the underworld.

Osiris sits as judge of the dead in the 'Hall of the Double **Maat**'.

Faience plaque with a man praying to Osiris.

The annual **festival** of Osiris lasted for a whole month. His death and resurrection were acted out in many different ways. Many temples had a 'tomb of Osiris' and mock **funerals** were held there for the god. Another festival custom was to make 'corn-mummies', which were mummy-shaped frames filled with soil. Grains of barley or corn were planted in the soil and the mummies were buried in **cemeteries**. When it rained the seeds would sprout and bring the corn-mummies to life. Osiris had become the god of agriculture and the corn was said to be his body. He suffered every summer when the corn was cut down and ground into flour, but he rose again every spring as the new corn grew.

Ostraca

Pieces of stone or broken pottery used for writing or drawing on (see **Letters** and **Painting and drawing**).

Egyptian artists often made sketches on ostraca.

Painting and drawing

The first Egyptian artworks were rock drawings done by prehistoric hunters about 5000 BC. The artists made drawings of the animals they wanted to catch, as a kind of **magic** to bring them into their power. A lot of later Egyptian art was also magic in some way. **Tomb** paintings were meant to provide for the dead in the next world (see **Art**) and even the wall paintings in **houses** had little figures of gods to protect the people who lived there. Not only walls, but **coffins**, statues, **pottery**, **furniture** and household objects were painted. Painters usually learned their trade as boys. At first they helped by fetching water, grinding and mixing the colours, and chewing sticks to make brushes. As they grew more skilled they were given more responsible jobs. They practised drawing by making sketches on all kinds of materials – rock, flakes of stone, bits of broken pottery and scraps of **papyrus**. The colours they used still look bright today because they were made from minerals – carbon (soot) for black, gypsum (Plaster of Paris) for white, ochre (iron-rich earth) for red and yellow, and malachite and azurite (stones containing copper carbonate) for green and blue. A beautiful blue-green colour was made from powdered **glass**, and some paintings were even finished with paint made from lapis lazuli or **gold**.

Small objects were probably painted by just one artist but a team usually worked on large wall paintings. Strict rules controlled the measurements of important parts of the paintings, which were first drawn out on a board marked with a grid of squares. Then a draughtsman marked out a larger grid on the wall to be painted and used it to copy the original drawing, enlarging it at the same time. After the chief draughtsman had checked and corrected it, the outlines of the drawing were filled in with colour.

More skilled artists completed the details and the chief added the finishing touches after checking the work again.

Although Egyptian painters had to keep to strict rules about what they painted and the colours they could use, they were very good at observing nature and drawing the **birds**, **animals**, plants and people they saw around them. Sometimes the little sketches they did tell us more about ancient Egyptian life than the big paintings in tombs.

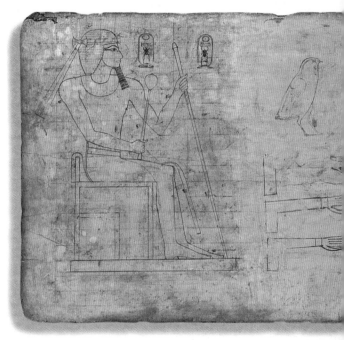

Draughtsman's board with a royal figure drawn onto a grid of squares.

Papyrus

Our word 'paper' comes from *papyrus*, the Latin word for the writing material made by the Egyptians from the stems of a tall reed called *cyperus papyrus*. Egypt was famous for its papyrus, which was one of the country's main exports. The papyrus plant flourished in the marshy Nile Delta and so became the symbol of Lower Egypt (see **Flowers**). Many temples had columns in the shape of papyrus stems (see **Architecture**).

Papyrus was made by peeling and soaking the stems of the reeds, and then slicing them into thin strips. The strips were beaten flat, then laid on top of each other in a criss-cross pattern and pressed under a heavy weight. By the time they were dry the strips had stuck together to form a strong sheet for writing. Several papyrus sheets were usually joined to make the scrolls used

Raw colours and a grindstone for preparing them..

Painting on papyrus showing the goddess **Hathor** as a cow surrounded by papyrus plants.

King Sety I offering incense to a god, using an incense burner like the one below.

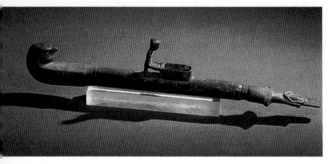

Bronze incense burner in the shape of a human arm and hand. Pellets of burning incense were placed in the palm of the hand.

for long texts like the **Book of the Dead**. In museums and libraries these book-scrolls are often called after the people who bought them, which is why they have names like 'Abbott Papyrus'.

Papyrus had lots of other uses. Bundles of stems could be tied together to make light boats for hunting and fishing, and sheets of papyrus were sometimes glued together in layers to make **cartonnage**, a kind of papier mâché used for **mummy** masks and cases.

Perfumes

The Egyptians loved sweet-smelling things of all kinds. They filled their houses with **flowers**, wore floral garlands and headdresses at parties, burned perfumed incense in their homes, and wore scented oils and ointments on their hair and skin.

Egyptian perfumes were famous throughout the ancient world. In **Graeco-Roman** times perfumes from the factories of **Alexandria** were exported all over the Mediterranean.

The perfumes were made from flowers like the lotus and the lily, fragrant woods like cedar and cinnamon, and resins like frankincense and myrrh. Many of these exotic ingredients were so rare and expensive that the factory workers had to take all their clothes off before they went home to prove they had stolen nothing!

Incense and perfumes also played an important part in religious rituals. Strong perfumes and incense offered at **funerals** were meant to stimulate the dead person's senses and help bring him or her back to life. In the **temples** huge amounts of incense were offered to the gods every day, and their statues were anointed with scented ointments (see **Abydos**). Some temples had special 'laboratories' where perfumes and incense were prepared from recipes carved on the walls. Some of the ingredients came from the temple **gardens**, but others had to be imported, and many pharaohs sent special missions to foreign lands to bring back spices, incense and myrrh as gifts for the gods (see **Trade**).

Pharaoh

A term used for Egyptian kings from the 15th century BC onwards. See **Kings**

Philae

The **Graeco-Roman** temple of **Isis** at Philae, just south of **Aswan**, guarded the border between **Egypt** and **Nubia**. People believed that the magical power of the goddess would protect Egypt from its enemies. The temple was built on an island in the middle of the Nile, close to another island where there was a shrine to Isis' husband **Osiris**. Philae was one of the most important pilgrimage centres in Egypt and the last Egyptian temple to remain in use. People worshipped there until the 6th century AD. Philae was flooded after the Aswan Dam was built, so in the 1970s the whole temple was taken apart like a giant jigsaw puzzle and moved to a safe place on another island nearby.

The temple of Isis at Philae as it is today, with the Aswan Dam in the background.

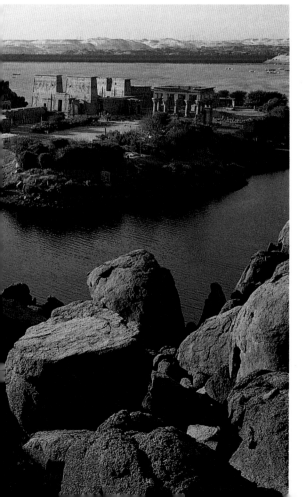

Pots

One of the first things the early Egyptians learned to do was to shape Nile mud and desert clay into waterproof containers. They soon found that baking their pots in fires made them harder. At first pots were modelled by hand, but by the end of the **Old Kingdom** they could be made much faster on potters' wheels. Potters later used special ovens called kilns to bake pots at higher temperatures, which made them even stronger.

The earliest Egyptian pottery was modelled by hand and baked in a fire. This polished jar was made about 4000 BC.

Pots were made in many different shapes and sizes, from tiny perfume containers to enormous storage jars for oil and grain. Pots for display were sometimes polished or painted with patterns. Some pots were even painted to look as though they were made of stone. If the pots broke, the pieces were useful for writing notes on. Fragments of broken pottery used for writing or drawing are called **ostraca**. Huge amounts of broken pottery have survived from ancient times, providing **Egyptologists** with many valuable clues as to how the ancient Egyptians lived.

Most pottery was undecorated, but some - like this jar for serving wine at parties ñ was painted.

Predynastic Period

(c.5500–3100 BC)

The slate palette of King Narmer.

A Predynastic pot showing people on a boat.

The deserts that surround Egypt were once grassy plains where many **animals** lived. The climate gradually became drier, so people came down from the plains to settle on the edges of the Nile Valley. The earliest known settlements date to around the 6th millennium BC. The Predynastic Period covers the many centuries between the founding of these settlements and the uniting of Egypt under **dynasties** of kings. Writing was only invented towards the end of this period, so there are few written records. More is known about southern Egypt than about the north. The culture of southern Egypt was very similar to that of **Nubia** for most of the Predynastic Period. The 4th millennium BC brought rapid changes. **Metal** tools and wonderful decorated **pots** began to be made. Walled towns were built and tribal leaders started calling themselves **kings**. Some of these early kings probably used the **gold** in Egypt's deserts to **trade** with more advanced civilizations, such as Mesopotamia (modern Iraq). The concepts of writing and of **building** in brick may have been borrowed from Mesopotamia, but the Egyptians developed them in a unique way.

In later times there was a strong tradition that the country had once been divided into two separate kingdoms of Upper Egypt (the south) and Lower Egypt (the north). Upper Egypt may have been united under one ruler in about 3250 BC and the culture of the south gradually spread north. The southern town of Hierakonpolis was very important at the end of the Predynastic Period. Beautifully carved objects such as ivory figurines and stone mace-heads and palettes (see **Cosmetics**) have been recovered from the early temple there. One palette names a King Narmer, the earliest king to be shown wearing the **crowns** of Upper and Lower Egypt. Narmer may be the same person as Menes, the legendary uniter of Egypt (see **Early Dynastic Period**).

Priests and priestesses

Priests and priestesses were rarely shown on the walls of ancient Egyptian temples. The **king** was officially the high priest of every temple, so he is the one shown serving the **gods**. In real life, however, many priests were needed to run the temples and take part in the daily services. The Egyptian title we usually translate as priest means 'god's servant'. An Egyptian priest's main duty was to look after the statue of the god in the temple (see **Temples**).

Priests were paid with shares of the **offerings** made in the temple. Many priests were only part-time and important people like **government** officials were often priests of the nearest major temple. Ordinary people did not go to the temples but served the gods in small local shrines. Some priests served more than one deity and each priest usually worked for one month in every four. At the end of each month a new shift took over. Priests were supposed to be good citizens but it wasn't part of their job to preach sermons or tell other people how to behave. When they were on duty in a temple they had to follow all sorts of rules to make themselves pure enough to serve the god. They had to live apart from their wives and avoid eating certain types of **food**, such as fish or pork. They were supposed to shave all the hair off their head and body and wear only clean **linen**. These rules were not always followed.

Only 'god's servants' were allowed to open the temple shrines and touch the divine statues. A lower grade of priests known as 'the pure ones' could carry the closed shrines around the temples during **festivals**. There were many special types of priest. Lector-priests could read and copy out the sacred books kept in temple libraries. 'Hour priests' watched the moon and the stars to help them predict the right time to hold festivals. 'God's singers' played the harp and sang during services. 'Ka priests' served the spirits of the dead (see **Afterlife**).

*A priest of **Thoth** carrying a sacred baboon.*

Single or married **women** could be 'god's servants' in the early days, and until about 1600 BC most noblewomen were priestesses of the goddess **Hathor**. They served part-time and, like the priests, they were paid. Priestesses later became rarer, but many women were involved in temple **music**. They sang or chanted hymns to the gods, played musical instruments, or performed **dances** during festivals. Some royal women became high priestesses of the god **Amun** and were treated as the wives of the god. At one period these 'God's Wives' ruled the south of Egypt like **queens**.

Ptah

Ptah was a creator god worshipped at **Memphis**. He was always shown as a bearded man wearing a tight-fitting cloak and a skull-cap, and holding a sceptre that combined the symbols for life, stability and power. The **priests** of Memphis claimed that Ptah had created the world 'by the thoughts of his heart and the words of his mouth'. Ptah was also the divine craftsman who made the bodies of the gods out of precious metals. He was said to have invented the 'Opening of the Mouth' ceremony, which was used to give life to statues and **mummies** (see **Funerals**).

At Memphis, Ptah was often paired with the lion-goddess **Sekhmet** and the lotus god Nefertem was their son. Ptah also had close links with Sokar, the falcon god of the **cemeteries** of Memphis, and later with **Osiris**. These three deities were sometimes thought of as one god, Ptah-Sokar-Osiris, the lord of the underworld. The main temple of Ptah at Memphis was one of the three most important temples in Egypt. **Kings** were often crowned there and the sacred **Apis bull** was kept nearby. There was a special area of the temple where ordinary people could come to pray to Ptah 'of the Hearing Ear'.

*The outer **coffin** of a high priestess of **Amun**.*

*The god **Ptah**.*

A temple relief showing King Ptolemy VIII and one of his queens.

A coin of King Ptolemy I, the founder of the dynasty.

Ptolemy

Ptolemy was the name of fifteen **Greek** kings who ruled Egypt from 305 BC to 30 BC – which is known as the Ptolemaic Period. Alexander the Great's empire began to break up after his death (see **Graeco-Roman Period**) and Ptolemy, the general who had been left in charge of Egypt, soon made himself king. Ptolemy I was an energetic ruler and much of the new capital city of **Alexandria** was built during his reign. He founded the famous library of Alexandria and built the great Pharos lighthouse that became one of the Seven Wonders of the Ancient World. During the 3rd century BC the Ptolemies conquered Cyprus and parts of Palestine and Syria.

The Ptolemies built fine **temples** to the gods of Egypt to please their Egyptian subjects. Despite this the Egyptians in the south of the country began to revolt at the end of the 3rd century BC. **Taxes** were heavy and a series of weak kings ruled after Ptolemy III. The Ptolemies became one of the unhappiest families known to history. The Ptolemy men married close relatives, who often became co-rulers of Egypt, and this frequently led to violent family feuds. Ptolemy IV married his sister and murdered his mother and his younger brother. Ptolemy VI had two queens: his sister Cleopatra II and his niece Cleopatra III. He murdered his son by Cleopatra II and sent her the body as a birthday present. Ptolemy XI married his aunt and then murdered her. He was killed by a mob after ruling for only nineteen days.

The Ptolemy women could be just as ruthless as the men. The famous **Cleopatra VII** had her sister executed and may have poisoned one of her brothers. By the time this Cleopatra became queen in 51 BC, the Ptolemies had lost their empire and her father, Ptolemy XII, had been forced to put Egypt under the protection of Rome. Cleopatra tried to make Egypt strong and independent again by forming alliances with the two greatest **Romans** of the age, Julius Caesar and Mark Antony. In the end she was defeated by Augustus, the future Emperor of Rome. Cleopatra's son Ptolemy Caesarion – who she claimed had been fathered by Julius Caesar – was killed by order of Augustus in 30 BC. Cleopatra's three children by Mark Antony were spared and one of them became queen of Mauretania (now Morocco). Cleopatra's youngest son, the last King Ptolemy, was murdered by his cousin, the Roman emperor Caligula.

Pylon

The term 'pylon', which is taken from a Greek word meaning 'gateway', is used to describe the entrance building of an Egyptian **temple**. A pylon is made up of a central doorway and two wide towers with sloping sides and flat roofs. Its shape is a bit like the **hieroglyph** for the horizon (see **Time**), and it may have represented the two mountains where the sun was thought to rise each day. Niches on the front held tall flagpoles representing protecting goddesses.

Ordinary people could not go inside the temple, so the pylon was one of the few parts of it that they saw. The kings knew this very well and usually made sure pylons were carved with scenes of them defeating Egypt's enemies. These carvings were supposed to give magical protection to the temple as well as impressing the king's subjects.

Pylon of the temple of Khons at **Karnak**.

Pyramids

A pyramid is a building with a square base and four triangular sides sloping inwards to meet in a pointed tip. More than eighty pyramids of different shapes and sizes have been discovered in Egypt. Most of them were built as royal **tombs** during the **Old Kingdom** and the **Middle**

The Old Kingdom ruler Sneferu built himself two pyramids at Dahshur, south of Saqqara. This one is usually called the 'Red Pyramid' because it is built from reddish-coloured limestone.

Kingdom. The pyramid, like the **obelisk**, had a strong influence on later architects all over the world. Rich Europeans from Roman times onwards have built themselves pyramid tombs, and today the pyramid shape is used for all kinds of buildings from greenhouses to hotels.

Throughout history people have been fascinated by the mysterious Egyptian pyramids and invented strange theories about them. Early Christian pilgrims thought they were the granaries where **Joseph** stored grain to feed Egypt during its years of famine. To the medieval Arabs they were stores of hidden treasure. In the 19th century European 'pyramidologists' interpreted their dimensions as a coded history of the world, and even today some people believe that they were built by aliens from another planet as landing markers for their spaceships!

The very first pyramid (and the first monumental stone building anywhere in the world) was the Step Pyramid at **Saqqara**, built for King **Zoser** in about 2650 BC. Although most later pyramids have square bases, the Step Pyramid is rectangular because it began as a **mastaba** tomb like the ones built for Egypt's first **kings**. At first Zoser's architect **Imhotep** enlarged the original mastaba, then he began adding more layers to create a stepped pyramid. Nobody is really sure why this shape was chosen. Some **Egyptologists** think that it reminded the

Egyptians of the Primeval Mound of the **creation myths**, others that it might have been meant as a staircase for the dead king's soul to climb up to heaven and join the sun and stars. The Pyramid Texts, magic spells carved in the burial chambers of later pyramids, often mention the king sailing in the **boat** of the sun god **Ra**.

In later pyramids the stepped sides were made smooth and the burial chamber was moved from under the ground to the pyramid's interior. The pyramid also became part of a whole complex of buildings meant to protect the dead king and help him on his journey to the **afterlife**. Beside the pyramid was a mortuary temple where **offerings** could be made to the king's spirit. This was joined by a covered passage, called a causeway, to a waterside temple known as the valley temple. This temple was where the king's body was received by the **priests** and prepared for burial. When the rituals had been completed the royal **mummy** was carried along the causeway to be laid to rest in a stone sarcophagus (see **Coffins**) deep inside the pyramid. Finally the passages leading to the burial chamber were sealed with heavy stone slabs to stop anyone getting in. Next to the king's pyramid there were often smaller pyramids for royal wives, mothers and daughters. The whole complex was enclosed by a high wall to stop people looking in.

The biggest and most famous pyramid is the Great Pyramid of **Khufu** at **Giza**, built in about 2570 BC. Its ancient name was 'The Pyramid which is the Place of Sunrise and Sunset', and it was one of the Seven Wonders of the Ancient World. It was almost 150 m (450 ft) high, and its sides were covered with gleaming white polished limestone. The capstone at the very tip was covered with gold to reflect the rays of the sun. Over 2,000,000 stone blocks, with an average weight of 2.5 tonnes, were used to build it. To this day nobody knows how the Egyptians were able to lift these huge stones into place. People have carried out experiments using the most likely methods – earth ramps, cranes and levers – but nothing has been proved.

However it was done, building pyramids this way obviously used too much labour, **stone** and time, because no more large stone pyramids were built after the 4th **Dynasty**. Late Old Kingdom pyramids were built of rubble covered or 'cased' with stone, and by the **New Kingdom** they were already falling apart. Inscriptions on some of the Saqqara pyramids tell how **Rameses II**'s son Khaemwaset found them in disrepair and had them mended. Middle Kingdom pyramids were even more fragile. They were often built over a mud-brick core and most have collapsed in ruins. Pharaohs began to be buried in rock-cut tombs in the **Valley of the Kings** during the New Kingdom and the only later royal pyramids were built in **Nubia** for the kings of Napata and Meroë.

A pyramid complex:

1. Pyramid tomb
2. Mortuary temple
3. Causeway
4. Valley temple

Queens

The English language uses the word 'queen' for women who rule a country and women who are married to kings, but the ancient Egyptians used different terms. The few women who ruled Egypt were given the same titles as **kings**. A 'King's Daughter' might become sole ruler if there was no suitable male heir. The **Old Kingdom** probably ended with a queen, and the last ruler of the 12th **Dynasty** was a Queen Sobekneferu. There were at least two female rulers in the **New Kingdom**. Queen **Hatshepsut**, who took the throne from her stepson, is usually dressed as a man in images that show her performing royal duties. The last ruler of the 19th Dynasty was Queen Tawosret, who had a fine decorated tomb in the **Valley of the Kings**. Southern Egypt was later ruled by High Priestesses of royal birth – these 'God's Wives' wore **crowns** and wrote their names in **cartouches**. In the **Graeco-Roman Period** many women of the **Ptolemy** family ruled Egypt jointly with their husbands or sons. The most famous of these was **Cleopatra VII**.

An Egyptian king might marry foreign princesses or daughters of Egyptian courtiers or nobles. The chief queen was known as the 'Great Royal Wife' and she was usually a close relative of the king. In Egyptian mythology **gods** often marry their sisters, and since Egyptian kings were supposed to be gods, they were also allowed to marry their sisters or half-sisters. Some kings even married their own daughters. The Great Royal Wife had much power and influence and was often shown standing next to the king. One of the titles of Queen **Nefertari** was 'She speaks and it is done'. Chief queens wore crowns that linked them with goddesses. They took part in many religious ceremonies, acting the roles of goddesses. Some Great Royal Wives even had **temples** built for them. During the New

Kingdom many royal wives were buried in the **Valley of the Queens**.

The eldest son of the Great Royal Wife was usually the heir to the throne, though a lesser wife sometimes gained power and respect as the 'King's Mother' if her son became the new ruler. Kings often put up statues to their mothers and built them fine **tombs** or memorial temples.

A king's wife of the **New Kingdom**.

A cylinder seal of Queen Sobekneferu, who ruled Egypt at the end of the **Middle Kingdom**.

R

The god Ra appears as a falcon-headed man wearing a sun disc.

This painting shows Ra-Horakhty, the morning sun.

Ra

Ra (or Re), the sun god, was usually shown as a falcon-headed man wearing a golden sun disc. As Ra-Horakhty he was the morning sun, and as Atum-Ra he was the evening sun. The names of other creator gods were linked to Ra because the sun was the greatest life-giving power known to the ancient Egyptians. They believed that **gods** were made from the sweat of Ra and that people were made from his tears. Ra lived in **Egypt** until humans began to plot against him, which made him so angry that he left the earth and made his home in the sky. Every day he crossed the sky in a **boat** rowed by gods and spirits. Every evening the sun was swallowed up by the sky goddess and entered the dark caverns below the earth.

Ra's temple at **Heliopolis** was one of the three most important **temples** in ancient Egypt. Egyptian **kings** called themselves sons of Ra from the time of the **Old Kingdom**, and in the 25th century BC several kings built temples for Ra on the edge of the desert. The focal point of these sun temples was a huge **obelisk**. In the **New Kingdom** royal **tombs** were decorated with scenes from the dangerous journey of the sun boat

through the underworld (see **Underworld Books**). During this journey the light of Ra was powerful enough to bring the dead back to life. Every evening the Egyptians prayed that the sun would come safely through the night. Every morning they greeted the sunrise with a hymn of praise.

Rameses II

Rameses was the name of eleven **New Kingdom** rulers. The most famous of these was Rameses II (c.1279–1213 BC). He was the grandson of a **vizier** who briefly became king after his royal master died childless. Rameses II seemed determined to outdo all previous rulers, perhaps because his family had not been born royal.

Egypt's empire in Syria and Palestine was threatened by the growing power of the Hittites (see **Egypt's neighbours**) and Rameses II led the **army** in person on several campaigns in Syria. The handsome young king must have looked very impressive with his pet lion by his side. During his second campaign, the Egyptians were ambushed by the Hittite army close to the city of Qadesh (see

Part of a colossal statue of King Rameses II.

Rameses III

Rameses III (*c*.1184–1153 BC) was the last great ruler of the **New Kingdom**. He was named after Rameses II but doesn't seem to have been related to him. **Egypt** had been through a brief civil war and was under pressure from the Libyans (see **Egypt's neighbours** and **Warfare**), but Rameses III soon defeated them and made thousands of them into **slaves**.

In the eighth year of his reign Egypt faced a terrible threat. One temple record says: 'The foreign lands plotted among their islands. The people were moved and scattered by war, all at once, and no country could stand before their weapons.' A vast invasion force known as the Sea Peoples (see **Egypt's neighbours**) swept towards Egypt. Rameses III rushed his troops to the north and defeated the invaders in land and sea battles.

A painting of Rameses III in the tomb of one of his sons.

The rest of his thirty-one-year reign was fairly peaceful. He added to many **temples** to thank the **gods** of Egypt for his victory. He also built a magnificent memorial temple to himself at **Medinet Habu**, where the walls are decorated with reliefs showing his battles. Some of the more gruesome scenes show soldiers counting the hands and other body parts of dead enemies. Rameses III was staying at the palace next to this temple when one of his wives tried to murder him. Nearly everyone involved in this murder plot was sentenced to death (see **Law and order**). The king's **mummy** shows no signs of violence, which suggests that he may have been poisoned. This is the mummy usually copied by makers of horror films!

Warfare). Rameses insisted that it was his personal bravery that saved the Egyptian army from total destruction. Both sides claimed Qadesh as a victory, but several years later Rameses decided to make peace with the Hittites. He married a Hittite princess as part of the peace treaty. Rameses II had many wives, but his favourite was Queen **Nefertari**. He seems to have been the father of at least 120 children.

Egypt was peaceful and prosperous for most of Rameses II's long reign and he added to or restored almost all the **temples** in Egypt. His huge memorial temple at **Thebes** is known as the **Ramesseum**. He also built a series of temples in **Nubia**, including the great rock-cut temples at **Abu Simbel**. Scenes of his 'victory' at Qadesh were carved on many temple walls and he built a whole new capital city called Piramesse in the Delta. By the end of his reign the old king was crippled by arthritis and could hardly walk. Many of his sons had died before him and their vast **tomb** in the **Valley of the Kings** is only now being explored. About 150 years after his death the **mummy** of Rameses II was moved to a secret place to save it from **tomb robbers**.

The colossal bust of Rameses II, now in the British Museum, being removed from the Ramesseum in 1816.

Ramesseum

The Ramesseum, the memorial **temple** of **Rameses II** on the west bank of the Nile at **Thebes**, was known to **Greek** and **Roman** tourists as the 'Tomb of Ozymandias'. (Ozymandias was how they heard Rameses' coronation name, Usermaatra.) The temple's most famous feature was a colossal statue of Rameses, and when a large bust of the king from the Ramesseum was brought to the British Museum in 1818 it inspired the Romantic poet Shelley to write *Ozymandias*, one of the most famous poems in the English language.

zymandias

I met a traveller from an antique land
Who said: Two vast and trunkless legs of stone
Stand in the desert. Near them, on the sand,
Half-sunk, a shattered visage lies, whose frown,
And wrinkled lip, and sneer of cold command,
Tell that its sculptor well those passions read
Which yet survive, stamped on these lifeless things,
The hand that mocked them and the heart that fed;
And on the pedestal these words appear:
'My name is Ozymandias, king of kings;
Look on my works, ye Mighty, and despair!'
Nothing beside remains. Round the decay
Of that colossal wreck, boundless and bare
The lone and level sands stretch far away.

Romans

The Romans thought of **Egypt** as an exotic and mysterious place, full of strange customs and incredibly ancient buildings. They mocked the Egyptians for worshipping animal-headed **gods** but envied them for their wealth. During the

A painted portrait replaces the traditional mask on many **mummies** of the Roman Period.

2nd century BC Egypt was ruled by a series of weak kings from the **Ptolemy** family (see **Graeco-Roman Period**). When there was a civil war between two Ptolemy brothers, Ptolemy VI and Ptolemy VII, both sides asked Rome for help. A delegation from Rome settled the dispute but the Romans then felt free to interfere in Egyptian politics.

King Ptolemy XII fled to Rome when the people of **Alexandria** rioted against him in the 1st century BC. The king borrowed an army from the Romans to fight members of his own family, and when he was back in power he made the leaders of Rome the legal guardians of his heirs, Ptolemy XIII and **Cleopatra VII**. Ptolemy XIII refused to share the throne with his sister. By this time a war was being fought between Rome's two greatest generals, Pompey and Julius Caesar. Pompey landed in Egypt in 48 BC to raise money to pay his troops, but the Egyptians had him murdered and sent his head to Julius Caesar. Caesar went to Egypt where he met and was fascinated by the young Cleopatra. He took her side against her brother during a fierce civil war. Cleopatra was soon restored to power and she and Caesar are said to have gone on a romantic cruise up the Nile. The next year she gave birth to a son, claiming that Caesar was his father.

Cleopatra was staying in Rome when Julius Caesar was murdered. She soon formed a relationship with another Roman general, Mark Antony, and helped him to pay his armies. In return Antony promised her that Alexandria would be the capital of a great new empire. Most Romans turned against Mark Antony when he divorced his Roman wife to marry Cleopatra. Antony and Cleopatra were defeated by Octavian, who later became Augustus, the first emperor of Rome. After this, Egypt was ruled by Roman governors. Greek and Egyptian continued to be the main languages of the country, but Roman law was imposed. Egyptian farmers were heavily taxed and much of their produce was exported to Rome. The growing population of the city of Rome soon came to rely on grain from Egypt. The Romans also mined for **gold** and precious **stones** in Egypt's deserts and built new ports on the Red Sea coast.

Many Roman citizens came to live in

*Bronze head of the Emperor Augustus found in **Nubia**.*

Egypt. The Roman poet Juvenal was exiled there for a time, but he hated the country and was rude about it in his poetry. Other Roman settlers were more interested in Egyptian culture. Some worshipped the goddess **Isis** and copied Egyptian burial customs. People buried in the Roman Period often had an Egyptian-style **coffin** but with a Roman-style portrait replacing the **mummy** mask. We know that visiting the ancient monuments of **Thebes** and **Memphis** became a popular pastime because some of these early tourists left graffiti in **tombs** and on statues. Lots of private **letters** survive from the Roman Period. They tell us about ordinary people worried about absent relatives, unhappy love affairs or high **taxes**. One Roman soldier complains that people are laughing at him because his mother hasn't sent him any clean underwear. In another letter a man writes to his pregnant wife that he is looking forward to the new baby, but only if it is a boy.

Rosetta Stone

The Rosetta Stone is a broken granite slab covered with inscriptions. It does not look very impressive but it was the key to unlocking the mysteries of ancient Egypt. The stone was discovered by a French soldier in 1799 at a place called Rosetta. Inscribed on the stone is a decree of the young King **Ptolemy** V, dated to 196 BC. What made the Rosetta Stone so exciting was that the same inscription was written in three versions. The first two versions were in ancient Egyptian but in different scripts: hieroglyphic and demotic. The third version was in Greek. Many scholars knew ancient Greek, but no one had been able to decipher Egyptian hieroglyphs.

After the British defeated the French general Napoleon, the Rosetta Stone was taken to the British Museum in London. Many European scholars studied and compared the three inscriptions, using copies of the stone. Several of them realized that the royal names they could read in the Greek text must be the words enclosed in **cartouches** in the hieroglyphic text. A Frenchman, Jean-François Champollion, used the Rosetta Stone and other royal inscriptions to show how the hieroglyphic script worked (see **Hieroglyphs and writing**). This made it possible for the ancient Egyptian language to be studied and understood. People now come from all over the world to see the Rosetta Stone.

The Rosetta Stone inscribed in hieroglyphic, demotic and Greek script. The stone has recently been cleaned.

Sacred animals

The ancient Egyptians saw awesome qualities in some **animals**. They admired the strength and cunning of a crocodile, the power and energy of a bull and the maternal devotion of a cow. They believed that the soul of a god or goddess could live for a while in the body of an animal. From very early times some **temples** chose one animal, bird or reptile to represent their deity and these sacred animals were treated like living statues of the god or goddess.

The most famous sacred animals were the Mnevis bull, which lived at **Heliopolis**, and the **Apis bull**, which lived at **Memphis**. Small herds of sacred cows were kept at several temples of the cow goddess **Hathor**, where they were looked after by special **priests**. This did not mean that all cattle were sacred and untouchable, however. Beef was the favourite meat of wealthy Egyptians and it was offered to the gods in temples (see **Food and drink**). It was a serious crime to kill a sacred animal but the Egyptians were not vegetarians and they enjoyed **hunting** animals.

Sacred animals were quite rare for most of Egyptian history. During the 1st millennium BC animal cults became much more important and whole species came to be thought of as semi-divine. All **cats** were sacred to **Bastet** and all ibises were sacred to **Thoth**. Foreigners thought this the oddest of all Egyptian beliefs. Sacred animals, birds or reptiles were usually kept in special enclosures close to temples but they weren't always properly cared for. One man wrote to the king to complain that priests were stealing the money they were supposed to spend on feeding the sacred ibises of **Saqqara**. Ordinary people tried to please the gods by feeding sacred animals and paying for them to be buried in special **cemeteries**.

Burying a sacred animal was an expensive business. The body was mummified, sprinkled with perfumed oils, wrapped in **linen** bandages and placed in a pot, box or animal-shaped coffin. These **coffins** range in size from tiny bronze ones for shrews to 2-tonne **stone** coffins for bulls. X-rays of these often show that the animal's neck had been broken. Sacred animals were also sacrificed to the gods. About 2,000,000 ibis and hawk burial places have been found at Saqqara. Many of the pots and boxes in which the birds were buried only contained a few stray bones bulked out with sawdust and bandages to look like a full **mummy**. The priests in charge were probably cheating by making several people pay for burying one sacred bird.

*Part of an underground burial area for ibises and baboons at Tura el-Gebel, the cemetery of **Hermopolis**.*

*Mummy of a sacred **cat** with decorative bandages.*

Saqqara

Saqqara, which is one of the most important sites in Egypt, was part of the royal cemetery of **Memphis**, Egypt's first capital. It lies in the desert to the west of the city and covers an area of more than 6 square km (3.75 square miles). Saqqara's earliest monuments are the **mastaba** tombs of Egypt's first rulers, the kings of the 1st and 2nd **Dynasties**. In the 3rd Dynasty King **Zoser** had his tomb, the Step Pyramid, built at Saqqara.

The Step Pyramid, which was built around 2650 BC, was the first **pyramid** in Egypt and the first monumental stone building in the world. It was built of small limestone blocks and had an underground burial chamber lined with granite. The corridors around the chamber were decorated with wall carvings of the king and panels of blue tiles. Next to the entrance on the northern side there was a sealed chamber called a *serdab* (Arabic for 'cellar') which contained a statue of Zoser. Two holes drilled in the wall of the chamber allowed the dead king's spirit to 'see' out through the statue's eyes. Zoser's other funerary buildings included halls and courts, and a temple for making **offerings** to the king's spirit. The whole complex was enclosed by a 10-m (30-ft) high wall to stop people from looking in.

Many pharaohs of the 5th and 6th Dynasties also chose Saqqara for their pyramids. Although these are smaller than earlier pyramids their interiors are carved with elegant **hieroglyphic** inscriptions known as the Pyramid Texts. Close by are the mastabas of royal relatives and courtiers, which are famous for their beautiful wall carvings. **New Kingdom** kings were buried in the south of Egypt at **Thebes** but many nobles still chose Saqqara for their **tombs**. Horemheb, the last ruler of the 18th Dynasty, had a large chapel tomb built there before he became king, and

The Step Pyramid of King Zoser at Saqqara.

Khaemwaset, High Priest of Ptah and son of **Rameses II**, was buried there alongside the sacred **Apis bulls** he served. During the **Graeco-Roman period** Saqqara became an important pilgrimage centre, and it remained in use as a cemetery up to the arrival of Christianity.

Sarcophagus

An outer coffin usually made of stone (see **Coffins**).

Scarab

Scarabs were the most common of all Egyptian **amulets**. Millions of them have been recovered from ancient sites and millions more are made today to sell to tourists. A scarab is a model of the African dung-beetle. This large black-green beetle shapes animal droppings into a ball, which it pushes along with its head and front legs.

Khepri, the god of the rising sun, was sometimes shown as a giant beetle pushing the sun out of the desert hills and across the sky. Stone statues of Khepri as a beetle were set up in some **temples**. A modern legend says that if

Back of a scarab representing the head and body of a dung-beetle.

you walk three times round the scarab statue at **Karnak** you will be granted a wish. Khepri was also the god of changes and transformations. The scarab became a symbol of the Egyptian hope that everyone who passed through the great change of death would be transformed into a spirit (see **Afterlife**).

Some scarabs are very realistic, while others are little more than an oval shape divided into a head and a body. The flat underside is often carved with words or images. From around 2000 BC many scarabs were inscribed with the name of the reigning king and were used to stamp the royal name on the clay seals that fastened **letters**, boxes and doors. Jars of wine or beer were also 'date-stamped' with scarabs.

Other scarabs were inscribed with good wishes or lucky mottoes and given away as presents. Simple scarab-shaped beads were made into cheap necklaces, while scarabs made from **gold** or lapis lazuli were used in royal **jewellery**. Some large scarabs were made for special reasons, such as commemorating royal events (see **Amenhotep III**) or protecting the heart of a dead person. Scarab amulets were hung round the necks of **mummies** or sewn onto their **linen** wrappings.

Scribes' palettes had a groove to hold their reed pens and wells for tablets of ink.

Scribes

Scribes were the civil servants of Egyptian **society**. They were essential to the running of the state. They were involved in everything from copying out religious texts and filing diplomatic **letters** to collecting **taxes**, paying workers, recording court cases (see **Law and order**) and organizing **building** projects and trading expeditions (see **Government**). A good scribe could be promoted to the highest offices in the land, so parents were keen to see that their sons got a good **education** to set them on the path to a successful career.

As well as learning to read and write in ancient Egyptian (see **Hieroglyphs and writing**) a trainee scribe might have to study foreign languages, **mathematics**, astronomy, geography or law, depending on his future post. His basic equipment consisted of an oblong palette with two round holes for cakes of solid red and black ink, and a long groove to hold his reed pens. He also had a small pot for the water used to wet the ink, a knife for trimming the sheets of **papyrus** he wrote on and a stone for smoothing its surface.

The god **Thoth** was the scribe of the gods and the patron of scribes. Scribes prayed to him for success, and many images show scribes with a baboon or ibis, Thoth's **sacred animals**.

Advice to a schoolboy: *Be a scribe! It saves you from labour and protects you from all kinds of work. It spares you from using the hoe and the mattock, so that you need not carry a basket. It saves you from having to row a boat and spares you torment ... the scribe, he directs all the work in this land!*

Statue of a scribe seated cross-legged with his papyrus spread across his lap.

Sculpture

Sculpture, like much of Egyptian **art**, often served a magical purpose. The Egyptians made sculptures from a huge variety of materials including **stone**, wood and **metal**. Luckily they left lots of unfinished pieces that help us to work out how they were made.

Stone sculpture falls into two types, free-standing pieces such as statues, and wall carvings or 'reliefs'. Three-dimensional sculptures were made in a huge range of sizes, from tiny figures of gods carved from rare stones to the enormous **Sphinx** at **Giza** and the huge statues of kings that stood in front of their **temples** (see **Colossi of Memnon**). High officials were sometimes allowed to place statues of themselves in the temples. Statues were sometimes painted or decorated with ornaments of coloured stone, **glass** or metal.

Wall carvings were an important part of religious buildings. In **tombs** they magically provided for the dead person's needs in the **afterlife**. In temples they provided magical protection and recorded the temple rituals. There are two types of wall carvings: 'sunk reliefs', where the designs are cut into the surface of the stone, and 'raised reliefs', where the background is cut away so that the design stands out. Sunk reliefs were the quickest and cheapest to do. They look good in bright sunshine and were often used on the outside of buildings. Raised reliefs took more time and expense, and were usually saved for inner parts of the temple such as the sanctuary. We are used to seeing statues and reliefs in their natural stone colour, but they were originally painted in bright colours.

Most of the wooden sculpture that survives was made for tombs and includes statues of the tomb-owners,

*Raised relief of an **offering**-bearer.*

Sunk relief. An unfinished stela belonging to the sculptor Userwer. You can see the grid and partly-cut figures in the bottom left-hand corner.

Sculptors at work. The men at the top are carving djed **amulets**, while the sculptor at the bottom right puts the finishing touches to a **sphinx**.

figures of **gods and goddesses** and models of servants. The finest pieces were coated with plaster, painted and decorated with **gold**. Metals like bronze, gold and silver were usually used for small figures of kings and deities, which were first modelled in wax and then cast in a mould. The sacred images kept in temple shrines were often made of precious metals.

Sculptors had to work to strict rules of proportion, just as painters did. They planned their work by drawing it out on a squared grid and then transferring the design to the block of wood or stone to be carved. The grid was always being cut away, so it had to be redrawn many times before the piece was finished. After it was carved the sculpture could be polished and decorated. Sacred images were thought to have a life of their own once they had been completed, and a special 'Opening of the Mouth' ritual (see **Funerals**) was held to bring them to life.

Free-standing wooden sculpture of a **New Kingdom** nobleman.

Second Intermediate Period (c.1650-1550 BC)

Between two great eras of Egyptian power, the **Middle Kingdom** and the **New Kingdom**, came the Second Intermediate Period (13th-17th **Dynasties**). The central government gradually became weak under the kings of the 13th Dynasty and foreigners known as

*The **coffin** of a king who ruled the Theban area in the Second Intermediate Period.*

the Hyksos (see **Egypt's neighbours**) settled in parts of the Delta. The Hyksos fought from horse-drawn chariots and had better weapons than the Egyptians. They became so powerful that some Hyksos leaders began to call themselves kings. Meanwhile a new Egyptian dynasty sprang up in **Thebes** and power was soon divided between the Hyksos kings in the north and the Theban kings of the 17th Dynasty in the south. According to an Egyptian legend one of the Hyksos kings caused a war by complaining that the noise of the sacred hippos of Thebes was keeping him awake. Thebes was about 640 km (400 miles) from the Hyksos capital, Avaris, so this was probably his way of saying that the Thebans were getting too troublesome.

The war began in the reign of King Seqenenre Taa. The king must have been killed in one of the battles that followed because his **mummy** shows terrible knife and axe wounds. The next Theban king Kamose, who may have been Taa's son or brother, sailed down the Nile to attack Avaris. Kamose put up a **stela** in the temple at **Karnak**, recording his victories, but he died young, probably in battle. The new king Ahmose was only a boy, so his mother Queen Ahhotpe became queen regent. She continued the struggle against the Hyksos and may even have led the **army** in person. Ahmose finally drove the Hyksos out of Egypt and destroyed their strongholds in Palestine. Egypt was strong and united again. Ahmose was commemorated by the last royal **pyramid** built in Egypt.

Sekhmet

The goddess Sekhmet (or Sakhmet) was usually shown as a woman with the head of a lion or a lioness. Her name means 'The Powerful One'. At **Memphis** Sekhmet

A granite statue of the lioness-goddess, Sekhmet. This is part of a set of over 700 statues.

was honoured as the wife of the creator god **Ptah**. At **Thebes** she was worshipped as a form of Mut, the queen of the gods. One Theban temple once had a pair of Sekhmet statues for every day of the year. These statues can now be seen in museums all over the world.

The Egyptians probably knew that lionesses do more hunting than lions and the role of the lioness-goddess was to hunt down the enemies of her father, the sun god **Ra**. She was one of several goddesses known as the **Eye of Ra**. Once, when the sun god was angry with humanity he sent Sekhmet to destroy them and she killed half the people on earth before Ra changed his mind. Ra had to stop her from killing the rest, so he had 6,000 jars of red beer poured onto the ground. When Sekhmet saw the beer she thought that it was blood. She lapped it all up and got too drunk to remember her mission! Plague and other infectious diseases were thought to be 'messengers' of Sekhmet and many spells were used to protect people against them. The **priests** of Sekhmet treated the sick with medicine and **magic**.

Senusret III

Three kings of the 12th **Dynasty** were called Senusret, or Senwosret (see **Middle Kingdom**). The name is sometimes also given as Sesostris. King Senusret III (1874-1855 BC) changed the way that Egypt was governed by ending the power of the families who ran the provinces. He fought a war in Palestine and completed the conquest of **Nubia**, where he built a chain of fortresses along the Nile. An inscription recording one of his campaigns in Nubia says 'I carried off their women. I struck down their cattle, I reaped their grain and burned their fields'. Senusret III was much feared by his enemies and Egyptian poems compare him to **Sekhmet**, the goddess of plague and destruction.

Most Egyptian kings were shown as young and handsome, whatever they had really looked like, but statues of Senusret III have grim faces lined with age. He seems to have been buried under a pyramid at Dashur, where beautiful jewellery belonging to his wife has recently been found. Senusret III was worshipped as a god for centuries after his death and the Egyptians eventually forgot that there had been more than one King Senusret. All the achievements of the 12th Dynasty were credited to one Senusret.

A life-size statue of King Senusret III. Most kings of the 12th Dynasty were shown with sticking-out ears.

Serqet

Serqet (or Selkis) was the scorpion goddess. She was usually shown as a woman with a scorpion on her head, its tail raised ready to sting. Female scorpions are larger and more poisonous than males. Their stings cause pain and shortness of breath and can be fatal to **children**. The Egyptians believed that Serqet had power over the breath of life, so she was asked to help the dead

*Part of a magical **stela** with spells against scorpions.*

breathe again. She was one of the four goddesses who protected a dead person's **mummy** and vital organs, and so can be seen on the side of **coffins** and the chests that hold **Canopic jars**.

Serqet was one of the few deities who was strong enough to subdue the chaos monster **Apophis**, and she helped the goddess **Isis** by sending seven deadly scorpions to be her bodyguards. Egyptian **doctors** tried to use the power of Serqet to drive poisons or fevers out of their patients' bodies. The **government** employed 'scorpion charmers' to persuade scorpions to leave desert areas where **building**, quarrying, or mining was to be done. The Egyptians hoped that they could save themselves from scorpions by honouring Serqet.

Servants

Paintings and models in the **tombs** of rich Egyptians always show the tomb-owners being waited on by armies of servants. There were no labour-saving devices in ancient Egypt, and large households and country estates needed a lot of staff. Jobs to be done included shopping, cooking, cleaning, washing and mending, as well as tending the **gardens** and the **animals**, making bread and beer, and spinning and weaving **linen** cloth. Besides the household staff there were nurses and tutors for the **children** and maids who took care of their masters' and mistresses' hair, **clothes** and make-up (see **Cosmetics**).

Even ordinary housewives employed servants or **slaves** to help them with their daily tasks. Everyone

A wooden model of a servant girl carrying a tray of food on her head.

Servants waiting on nobles at a party.

in the household depended so much on each other that servants and slaves were treated as members of their employer's **family** and sometimes married into it.

Seth

The head of the mysterious 'Seth animal' has a long nose and ears.

Seth (or Sutekh) was the chaotic god of storms. He was one of the five children of the sky goddess and the earth god (see **Creation myths**) and was said to have torn his way out of his mother's stomach. Seth's birthday was one of the unluckiest days in the Egyptian calendar (see **Year**). The storms that sweep in from the desert can be very destructive – and so was Seth. He could take the form of many dangerous animals, such as the wild bull, the hippopotamus, or the crocodile, but he was usually shown as an imaginary beast with a long curved snout, tall ears, cloven hooves and a forked tail. This strange creature may be a mixture of a wild ass and an aardvark. Seth could also appear as a griffin, a monster that was part lion, part hawk and part snake. The deserts beyond Egypt's boundaries were thought to be full of such monsters.

Seth was the strongest of the gods but not the most intelligent. He was jealous of his brother **Osiris**, who had been chosen to rule Egypt, and so he murdered Osiris and also tried to kill his nephew **Horus**. Horus survived to fight Seth for the crown of Egypt and challenged him to a race in stone boats. Seth made a heavy stone boat, which sank at once. Horus' boat was only painted to look like stone, so he won the race. After many fights and arguments Horus became king and Seth was sent to live in the sky and be the god of thunderstorms. His great strength was needed to protect the sun god on his nightly journey through the underworld. Seth was sometimes shown in the prow of the sun boat, spearing or clubbing the chaos monster **Apophis**.

The most important **temple** dedicated to Seth was at Avaris in the north-eastern Delta. He was honoured in this region throughout the 2nd millennium BC but was later thought of as the leader of the forces of evil. Every year a festival was held at the temple of **Edfu** to celebrate the victory of Horus over Seth. The climax of this festival was the 'Cutting of the Hippopotamus Cake', when an image of Seth was sliced up and eaten. In the **Roman** Period Seth was often invoked in 'black magic'. Some of the imagery of the Devil of Christian tradition may be based on Seth.

The temple of Amun at Siwa.

Siwa

The ancient town of Siwa is built around an **oasis** deep in Egypt's western desert and even today it is difficult to reach. It was a holy place to the Libyans (see **Egypt's neighbours**) and the Egyptians. It had a famous **temple** where a mysterious image of the god **Amun** answered people's questions (see **Oracles**). In the 6th century BC a cruel Persian king called Cambyses conquered Egypt. He is said to have sent an army to capture Siwa and destroy the temple of Amun but this army disappeared in the desert before it reached the town. The Egyptians believed that Amun had raised a sandstorm to kill the Persian invaders.

About 200 years later the **Greek** general Alexander the Great conquered the Persian empire and came to Egypt. He made a dangerous three-week journey across the desert to Siwa to ask Amun a question. The high priest of the temple greeted Alexander as the son of Amun. Alexander refused to tell anyone what he had asked Amun but he did say that he had got the answer he wanted. Alexander seems to have believed that he was a god after his trip to Siwa, and that he could do anything. There is a local legend that the body of Alexander the Great was secretly reburied at Siwa centuries after his death and people still come to the town to search for him.

Slaves

The popular idea that the **pyramids** were built by slave labour is untrue. Slavery was not common in Egypt until long after the time of the pyramid builders. Most slaves were prisoners-of-war or foreigners sold into slavery by their own people, but sometimes very poor Egyptians sold themselves or their **children** so that they wouldn't starve. All prisoners taken during foreign wars belonged to the king and they were usually sent to work on royal estates or given to **temples**. Some soldiers were allowed to keep their captives as a special reward for bravery (see **Army**). Favoured **government** workers might be given a share of a slave's time as part of their wages. Many foreign women worked in Egyptian homes weaving **linen** or doing housework. These women often 'belonged' to the lady of the house.

Being a slave in Egypt meant that you had to work for the person who owned you. Most ancient Egyptians had little choice about where they worked or what jobs they did, so the difference between freeborn and slave workers may not have seemed very great. Slaves had many of the legal rights of free people. They were allowed to own property and marry a freeborn partner, and some slaves even married a member of the **family** they worked for. Others were adopted by their owners and became their heirs.

Tile from a royal palace, showing a Libyan captive. Prisoners-of-war were taken back to Egypt as slaves.

*On this **stela**, a group of men pray to a local snake goddess.*

Snakes

Many species of snake live in Egypt and some, like the cobra and the viper, are poisonous. An ancient Egyptian **papyrus** describes twenty-one different kinds of snake. The papyrus divides snake bites into three main types: bites that are harmless, bites that can be treated and bites where 'death comes quickly'. In Egyptian myth many supernatural beings had snake forms. The chaos monster **Apophis** appeared as a huge snake, probably a python, to attack the boat of the sun god (see **Underworld Books**). Wadjyt, the goddess who guarded northern Egypt, was a deadly marsh cobra (see **Two Ladies**). A snake goddess who lived on a holy mountain at **Thebes** was called 'She who Loves Silence', probably as a reminder that snakes hate

to be disturbed. The local people believed that if they made this snake goddess angry she would blind them.

Snakes were a danger to workers in the fields at harvest time but they did prey on the mice, sparrows and locusts that ate the crops, which may be why the harvest goddess Renenutet had the form of a cobra. Her name means 'the Snake who Nourishes'. **Pottery** bowls in the form of coiled snakes have been found in many ancient Egyptian houses, where they were probably used to offer milk or beer to the harvest goddess. Pairs of snakes were sometimes carved or painted on beds and chairs because the Egyptians hoped that images of snake deities would frighten off real snakes and any other harmful creatures that got into the house. Egyptian magicians used snake-shaped wands to protect people against demons and dangerous animals.

141

Sneferu

King Sneferu was born in the 27th century BC and ruled Egypt for at least twenty-four years. He was the first king to enclose his name in a **cartouche** and the first to build a true **pyramid**. Sneferu sent expeditions to **trade** for timber in Lebanon and mine for turquoise in Sinai. He was known as the 'Smiter of the Barbarians' and he fought against the **Nubians** and the Libyans (see **Egypt's neighbours**). Sneferu was one of Egypt's greatest builders. He seems to have finished building the pyramid of his father-in-law at Meidum and he built two pyramids for himself at Dashur. These are known as the Bent Pyramid and the Red Pyramid. More stone was used in these three pyramids than in the Great Pyramid built by Sneferu's son **Khufu**.

In Egyptian legend Sneferu was remembered as a man who liked to enjoy life. One story describes how he went for a trip on a lake in a **boat** rowed by twenty beautiful girls wearing see-through clothes. One of the rowers lost a turquoise **amulet** in the water and was too upset to go on. Sneferu offered to get her a new one but the rower wanted her own lucky amulet back. Instead of being angry, the kindly king sent for his court magician, who used a spell to roll back the waters of the lake and retrieve the amulet. Sneferu was delighted and ordered a great feast to celebrate. In another story Sneferu was entertained by listening to a wise **priest** who could foresee the future. The king insisted on writing down the priest's prophecy himself. These two stories were probably written over 700 years after Sneferu's death.

*The Bent Pyramid, one of several **pyramids** built by King Sneferu.*

Sobek

The god Sobek, who was shown as a crocodile or as a man with the head of a crocodile, was a powerful and frightening deity. In some myths it was Sobek who first came out of the waters of chaos to create the world (see **Creation myths**). As a creator god he was sometimes linked with the sun god **Ra**. Most of Sobek's **temples** were in parts of Egypt where crocodiles were common. One was at a place in the **Fayum** that the Greeks called Crocodilopolis ('Crocodile Town'). Another was at Kom Ombo, close to sandbanks in the Nile where crocodiles liked to bask.

*This gilt-bronze crocodile would have been an **offering** to Sobek.*

Egyptians who worked or travelled on the river hoped that if they prayed to the crocodile god he would protect them from being attacked by crocodiles. Some temples of Sobek had pools where sacred crocodiles were kept. These crocodiles were fed on the best cuts of meat and became quite tame. One ancient **Greek** writer even claimed that sacred crocodiles were given gold earrings and anklets to wear. When they died, they were mummified and buried in special cemeteries (see **Sacred animals**).

Society

Ancient Egyptian society was a bit like a pyramid. At the top was the pharaoh, the divine king, and beneath him were the members of the court: the high officials and the royal family. Next came the nobility: the priests, civil servants and landowners. Below them were the skilled craftspeople and traders. Finally, at the bottom, were the vast majority of the people: the peasants who worked the land. Although these people were not **slaves**, they were not free to leave the land they worked and were counted as part of the landowner's property. Foreigners were often treated differently from Egyptians. Greek traders in Egypt lived in their own towns, and the city of **Alexandria** had separate quarters for Egyptians, **Greeks** and Jews.

In some ways, though, Egyptian society was quite open and even peasants could own land and improve their status. **Education** was another important route to success. A clever boy who studied hard could go far in the civil service. But although a hard-working **scribe** could rise to a high post in the **government**, it was difficult to break into the top ranks of society, where the best jobs were usually kept within the same families. Sometimes an ambitious man's best career move was to marry his boss's daughter! Royal princesses sometimes married high officials, and if there was no heir to the throne the royal son-in-law might become king, especially if he already held a high position such as that of **vizier**. The Egyptians loved to hear rags-to-riches tales, just as people do today, and some of their most popular **stories** were about poor peasants who made their fortune through good luck and hard work.

*A sphinx statue guarding one of the **temples** of **Memphis***.

Sphinx

The **Greek** word sphinx may come from an Egyptian phrase that meant 'living image'. The earliest known ancient Egyptian sphinx statues date to the 26th century BC, but the most famous is the Great Sphinx that sits in front of the pyramids of **Giza**. There were many sphinx statues in ancient Egypt. They have the body of a lion and the head or face of some other creature. The most common combination was a lion's body with a human head, but sphinxes also had the heads of rams, hawks or even the **Seth**-monster. In ancient Greek myth sphinxes were female, but Egyptian sphinxes were usually male. They were thought to live in the remote desert and a giant, double-headed sphinx guarded the entrance to the underworld.

Sphinxes were usually given the face of the reigning king and the Great Sphinx is probably a portrait of King Khafra (Chephren). The striped royal headdress was sometimes replaced by a lion's mane

(see **Nubia**). The reigning king might also appear on **jewellery**, weapons and chariots as a sphinx trampling the enemies of Egypt. A few famous **queens** such as **Hatshepsut** and **Nefertiti** were shown as sphinxes. Sphinxes became a symbol of the duty and the power of the king or queen to protect Egypt.

The Egyptians believed that sphinx statues had magical powers to guard **temples** and **tombs**, and from the time of the **New Kingdom** some temples were approached by avenues or canals lined with sphinxes. By this time people were worshipping the Great Sphinx at Giza as a form of the sun god. It was also identified with a foreign god called Hauron who protected people from the dangers of the desert. In more recent times, people feared this statue as a demon.

Sports

The Egyptians considered that physical activity was very important for boys and young men because they might have to go and fight in the **army**. As boys they practised shooting at targets with bows and arrows, and tomb paintings also show young men performing gymnastic exercises, perhaps as a part of their army training. Competitive sports of all kinds were popular with men, and **festivals**

Painted clay model of wrestlers.

were celebrated with races, boxing and wrestling matches, stick-fighting, archery and tug-of-war contests, and even boat fights, when rival crews would try to sink each other. Although **women** do not seem to have participated much in sports, girls and young women are sometimes shown performing gymnastics and juggling with balls. In the **Graeco-Roman Period** spectator sports like chariot racing and gladiator fights became popular in large cities such as Oxyrynchus and **Alexandria**, and boys and young men could develop their athletic skills in gymnasiums.

foreigners that they were entering Egyptian territory. Ordinary people were sometimes allowed to put up stelae in or near temples. The person who paid for the stela was usually shown on it 'giving praise' to the god or goddess of the temple. Some stelae just show the ears of a god because people hoped that if they paid for an 'ear stela' the god would listen to their prayers.

Stela

A stela (or stele) is a stone or wooden slab that can either be rectangular or have a rounded or pointed top. Ancient Egyptian stelae have carved or painted scenes and inscriptions in **hieroglyphs** on one or both sides. The earliest stelae date to around 3000 BC and come from **cemeteries**. The custom of having a funerary stela continued until Egypt became a Christian country. Most funerary stelae were inscribed with the name of the dead person and prayers for their well-being in the **afterlife**.

Egyptian stelae were not always gravestones, however. Kings put up large stelae to record achievements such as winning battles or building **temples** and often placed stelae at border sites to warn

*A typical **New Kingdom** stela.*

Three deities (Osiris, Isis and Hathor).

Prayers to the gods for the spirit of the stela-owner.

*The stela-owner and his wife with a table of **offerings**.*

The stela-owner and his brother praying.

Their family.

Stone

The Egyptians used many different kinds of stone for **building**, **sculpture**, **jewellery** and decorating **furniture**. The main building stones were limestone, found in the north of Egypt, and sandstone, found in the south. Stone was usually quarried as close to the building site as possible to make transporting it easier, but good-quality stone sometimes had to come from further away. The most important limestone quarry, at Tura, near Cairo, provided the fine limestone used to cover the **pyramids** at **Giza**. The best sandstone came from Gebel el-Silsila near **Edfu** and was used to build many of the **temples** in the south. Shrines, statues and **obelisks** were often made from the beautiful black and red granite quarried at **Aswan**.

Stonemason's tools: a wooden mallet and chisels with bronze blades and wooden handles.

The granite quarries at Aswan.

Egyptian stone-workers were very skilled at shaping stone accurately with basic tools. They used translucent white alabaster for decorating buildings, creating elegant vases and boxes and making statues and **Canopic jars**. Semi-precious stones were used in jewellery and for decorating furniture and royal statues. Purple amethyst, green emerald, orange-red carnelian and clear quartz crystal all came from mines deep in the

Unfinished limestone statue of a queen or goddess.

deserts to the east and west of the Nile, while turquoise was mined in Sinai. The mines were sacred to the goddess **Hathor**, who was worshipped there as the 'Lady of Turquoise'. The most prized stone of all, dark blue lapis lazuli, had to be imported from far-off Afghanistan.

Softer stone such as limestone or sandstone was quarried using bronze tools, but granite had to be pounded out with hammers made from hard rock. Stoneworkers could then shape the stone with **metal** chisels or round hammer stones. Large objects like statues and sarcophagi (see **Coffins**) were often shaped from the rock before they were cut free from it. Quarried stone was usually taken to its destination by water. The best time to do this was during the annual Nile flood, when the high water let the sailors bring their barges close up to the building site. The final work such as carving inscriptions and polishing the stone with sand was done at the site.

Stories

Like people everywhere, the ancient Egyptians enjoyed a good story. Popular stories were retold over the centuries, and written down on **papyrus** and **ostraca**, scraps of broken pottery or stone.

A favourite type of story was about good but poor people winning over wealthy villains. In *The Tale of the Eloquent Peasant* a poor man's donkey is taken away by a wicked landowner because it eats some of the grain from his field. But when the case comes to court (see **Law and order**) the poor man's clever speeches delight the judges so much that they take away all the rich man's property and give it to the peasant.

Stories of adventure and foreign **travel** were always popular. A favourite tale, *The Story of Sinuhe*, tells how an Egyptian courtier runs away to another country in panic after the pharaoh is murdered. After many adventures he becomes chief of a foreign tribe and eventually returns to Egypt. The supervisor of the tomb-builders in the **Valley of the Kings** liked this story so much that he had a copy of it placed in his tomb to take with him to the **afterlife**, rather like we might take a good book on a long journey. If a travel story had **magic** in it, so much the better. *The Tale of the Shipwrecked Sailor* tells of a sailor who finds himself on a magic island after his ship is lost in a storm. The only living creature on the island is a giant talking serpent who looks after the man until a ship from Egypt comes and rescues him. After the ship sails away the island sinks into the sea and is never seen again!

Some Egyptian stories are quite like our fairy tales. In *The Tale of the Unlucky Prince* the Seven Hathors (like the fairy godmothers in *Sleeping Beauty*) foretell that a baby prince will die because of a **snake**, a crocodile or a **dog**. When the prince grows up he travels to Syria where he wins the hand of a beautiful princess. She saves him from the snake … but the end of the papyrus is missing, so we never find out how the story ends!

Papyrus with The Tale of the Unlucky Prince *written in hieratic script.*

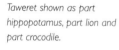

Taweret shown as part hippopotamus, part lion and part crocodile.

Nobody looked forward to the arrival of the tax collectors:

The tax-official has landed on the river bank to register the harvest tax, with the janitors carrying staves and the Nubians carrying palm rods. They say, 'Give up the grain!' even though there isn't any!

Taweret

The name Taweret means 'the Great One' and was a polite way to refer to a very frightening goddess who was one of the wives of the chaos god **Seth**. In her most common form she had the head and body of a hippopotamus, the paws of a lion and the tail of a crocodile. Sometimes she was shown with a whole crocodile attached to her back. The Egyptians chose these strange forms to show that Taweret had the strength of all these dangerous animals. Figures of Taweret often held knives, torches or a sign that meant 'protection'. She was one of a group of supernatural 'fighters' called on to protect women and children from attacks by demons and she appears with the lion-dwarf **Bes** on magical and household objects.

As a hippopotamus Taweret was linked with the power of the River Nile because she was the goddess of 'the Pure Waters' that gave life to Egypt. Vases in the form of the hippopotamus goddess were used to hold water or milk. Taweret also had a place among the stars. In Egyptian star-maps she is shown in the northern sky next to the 'Foreleg of Seth', which we call the Great Bear. A myth tells how Seth turned himself into a bull and trampled his brother **Osiris** to death. His leg was cut off as a punishment and placed in the heavens. Taweret was sent to guard the leg so that it could never harm anyone again.

Taxes

One of the reasons the Egyptian **government** could work so effectively was its efficient tax collection system. There was no money, so taxes were paid in goods such as grain, **linen** and livestock, and all farmers and landowners had to give some of their produce to the government. A census was held every

*Geese being counted for the census. On the left, a scribe records the numbers on a sheet of **papyrus**.*

two years to decide just how much this should be. **Scribes** were sent to each farm to measure the fields and count all the **animals** and **birds** in order to work out what each landowner had to pay. All the goods taken in payment were held in great stores at the **temples** and used for state purposes such as paying government employees. Anyone who didn't pay their taxes was taken to court (see **Law and order**). They were made to pay and quite often received a beating as well.

Temples

The most impressive buildings in ancient Egypt were the **tombs** of the **kings** and the temples of the **gods**. The earliest temples were small and made from reeds or mud-brick (see **Architecture**), but as time went on they got bigger and grander. Later temples were mainly built in **stone** and every surface was decorated with images of deities and kings. The basic elements of an Egyptian temple were an enclosure wall, a courtyard, an offering room and a sanctuary. Everything inside the enclosure wall was sacred ground but the sanctuary was the holiest part of the temple. From the **New Kingdom** major

The memorial temple of King **Rameses II** surrounded by brick storerooms and granaries.

temples had massive **pylon** gateways and great **hypostyle halls** supported by decorative columns.

The Egyptians believed that it was very important to please the gods by giving them splendid homes to live in and plenty of **offerings**. Every temple was the mansion of a particular god or goddess, or of a family of deities. People thought that the spirit of the main deity inhabited a statue kept in the sanctuary. Sanctuaries were always quite small and dark and the god's statue was kept

hidden inside a wooden shrine. **Priests and priestesses** brought the statue new food, clothing and **cosmetics** every day (see **Abydos**). The temple choir sang hymns to it every morning. Pictures of these rituals on the temple walls could act as magical substitutes for the real thing (see **Art**).

Egyptian temples did not have a congregation, as a church or a mosque or a synagogue does. The only people who could enter the sanctuary were the king and high-ranking priests or priestesses. Ordinary people had to pray in the courtyard in front of the temple, or even outside the enclosure wall. This rule was

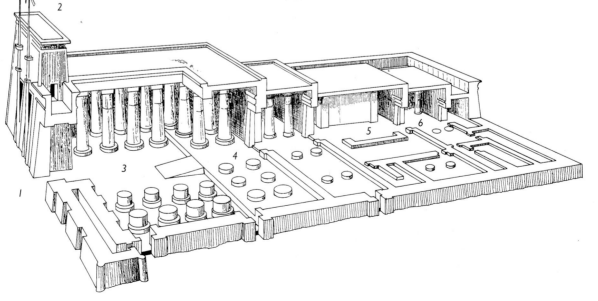

Cross-section of one of the temples at **Karnak**:

1. Main courtyard
2. Flagpoles and pylon gateway
3. Pillared courtyard
4. Columned hypostyle halls
5. Sanctuary with shrine for the god's statue
6. Anterooms

149

sometimes relaxed during special religious **festivals**.

People were not buried in temple grounds during most of Egyptian history, but the spirits of the dead could live in statues set up in temples. The chief deity of some temples was a dead king or queen. After a ruler was buried in his tomb, offerings were made to his spirit in a nearby temple. Until the 15th century BC most royal temples were very close to the tomb itself (see **Pyramids**). During the New Kingdom large memorial temples were built some distance from the royal

*A **king** offering wine to a god as part of the daily ritual.*

tombs in the **Valley of the Kings**. These temples were shared between the dead rulers and important local deities.

The major temples were supported by the state with grants of land and goods. They were like small towns with houses for priests and offices for administrators clustered around the main buildings. Some temples ran schools to train **scribes** and had excellent libraries where people studied subjects like medicine, astronomy and **magic**, and books were copied by hand. Law courts often met in temple courtyards so that the gods would see justice done (see **Law and order**). **Taxes** paid in grain were stored in temple granaries and redistributed as wages. Skilled craftsmen made statues, **furniture**, textiles and **jewellery** in temple workshops and beautiful objects such as painted **coffins** could be bought there. Some temples also employed thousands of people to work on their farmlands. For all these reasons, the local temple was the centre of the community. When Egypt went through troubled times kings built or rebuilt temples to help the economy and please the gods.

Great temples such as **Karnak** were never really finished because each king tried to add something so that the gods would bless his reign. This could be anything from a statue or a piece of furniture to a whole new building. Kings hoped that such gifts would keep their own memory alive.

The ruined temples of Egypt are still awe-inspiring but they must have been even more impressive when their walls were brightly painted, their doors were covered with silver and **gold**, and their rooms were perfumed with incense and filled with **music**. There is a legend that if the temples of Egypt cease to exist, the world will end.

*The temple of **Khnum** at Esna, one of the last Egyptian-style temples ever built.*

Thebes

Thebes was the **Greek** name for the ancient town of Waset, one of the most important cities of ancient Egypt. Its modern name, Luxor, came from the first Arabs who went there. When they saw the remains of its great **temples** they called them 'el-Uqsur', which means 'The Palaces'. Thebes first became important during the **Middle Kingdom** when the 11th-**Dynasty** kings chose it as their capital. The earliest large-scale **building** there was done by Nebhepetra Mentuhotep, who built himself a spectacular funerary monument, half-tomb and half-temple, at **Deir el-Bahri** on the Nile's west bank. The royal palace was directly opposite, at **Karnak** on the east bank. Over the centuries kings added their own palaces on both sides of the river, and the homes of the nobility and the working people who served them sprang up all around. Thebes was at the height of its power during the **New Kingdom**, when the local god **Amun** became the chief state god. By the **Late Period** the royal residence had returned to the north, but the whole of southern Egypt was ruled from Thebes by a powerful dynasty of priestesses known as the 'God's Wives of Amun'.

The city's **cemeteries** were scattered among the limestone cliffs on the west bank of the Nile. Throughout the New Kingdom, kings were buried in rock-cut **tombs** hidden deep in the **Valley of the Kings**, while **offerings** to their spirits were made in memorial temples built along the edge of the desert at sites like Deir el-Bahri, **Medinet Habu** and the **Ramesseum**. Queens, princes and

Ancient Thebes.

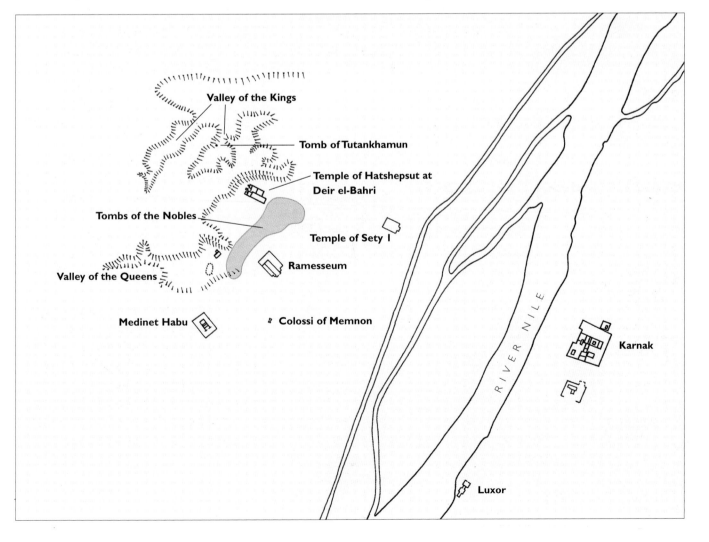

Luxor temple.

princesses were buried in the **Valley of the Queens**. The royal tomb-builders lived in the nearby village of **Deir el-Medina**, surrounded by the tombs of their ancestors. Every year, during a festival called 'The Beautiful Festival of the Valley', the people of Thebes dressed in their best clothes and sailed across the river to spend the night feasting at their relatives' tombs.

The god of Thebes was Amun, who was worshipped with his wife Mut, their son Khons and the local war god Montu. Construction of the great Temple of Amun at Karnak was begun during the Middle Kingdom and extended over the next 2,000 years. Each year, during the Opet festival, the divine images were taken by river from Karnak to Amun's 'Southern Harem' at Luxor temple. Luxor temple, which was begun in the New Kingdom, has served many faiths. In **Roman** times soldiers stationed near the

temple built a chapel to their divine emperors, and in Christian times it was used as a church. Today a mosque built over part of the temple serves Luxor's Muslim population.

Third Intermediate Period (*c.*1069–664 BC)

By the end of the **New Kingdom** the kings of the 20th **Dynasty** were living in the Delta and had little control over the south of Egypt. The High Priests of the god **Amun** at **Thebes** started to call themselves **kings**, and power was soon divided between the priest-kings in the south and a new line of kings, the 21st Dynasty, at Tanis in the north. It would be nearly 300 years before Egypt was really united again.

The 22nd Dynasty took over in the north in the 10th century BC. These kings

The High Priest Herihor and his wife are shown as a **king** and **queen** in this Third Intermediate Period papyrus.

were descended from Libyan families (see **Egypt's neighbours**) who had been resettled in the Delta. King Sheshonq I forced the Thebans to accept his own son as High Priest of Amun and then tried to recover parts of Egypt's former empire by winning victories in **Israel and Judah**. The rulers of the 21st and 22nd Dynasties brought statues, columns and **obelisks** from several sites in Egypt to decorate their capital city. Many **gold** and silver treasures have been found in their **tombs**.

The power of the kings was growing weaker and local governors in the cities were increasing their authority. Sometimes this led to conflict. By the 8th century BC rival dynasties of kings had sprung up in several parts of Egypt. Kings of the 22nd and 23rd Dynasties tried to control Thebes by making their daughters high priestesses and 'God's Wives of Amun' (see **Queens**). The God's Wife ruled most of the south like a queen but

Egypt was still divided. Change came in an unexpected way. Egypt had always had a great influence on the neighbouring country of **Nubia**. During the Third Intermediate Period Nubia was ruled from the city of Napata. The Napatans had a strong culture of their own but they worshipped Egyptian gods.

A Napatan king called Piy (or Piankh) was a devoted follower of Amun and made the Thebans accept his sister as the next God's Wife of Amun. In the 8th century BC King Piy invaded Egypt and forced all the local rulers to pay homage to him. When some of them later rebelled King Piy 'raged like a panther'. He led his army north and captured all the main cities, punishing one of the rebel kings for allowing his horses to starve during a siege. Egypt was soon united again under the strong rule of the Napatan kings of the 25th Dynasty. This new era is known to historians as the **Late Period**.

153

Thoth

Thoth was the god of knowledge and wisdom and was also a moon god. His **sacred animals** were the baboon and the ibis, a long-necked bird. He was shown as a baboon, an ibis or an ibis-headed man and in all these forms he often wore a headdress with a full moon above a crescent moon.

Thoth was the patron god of **scribes** because the Egyptians said that he had invented **hieroglyphs and writing**. He was often shown carrying a scribe's writing kit and scenes of scribes at work sometimes have a statue of him in a corner of the office. In his role as recorder of the gods, Thoth wrote down what every person's fate was and how long they were going to live. He was also in charge of secret knowledge and **magic**. The Egyptians told **stories** about the mysterious 'Book of Thoth'. Its spells were so powerful that they could enchant the earth and the sky and everything in them. They believed that Thoth used his magic to protect the body of **Osiris** and to heal the wounded **Eye of Horus**.

The **Greeks** identified Thoth with their god Hermes and his greatest temple was at the place the Greeks called **Hermopolis**. Little is left of this temple today except for two colossal stone baboons. A local legend claimed that the temple was built on the very spot where the sun god hatched from an ibis egg. In a nearby cemetery there are tunnels full of mummified ibises and baboons and at **Saqqara** priests of Thoth looked after thousands of sacred ibises (see **Sacred animals**). In **Roman** Egypt Thoth the 'Three Times Great' was worshipped as the wisest of gods and people hoped that he would teach them all the secrets of the universe.

*An **amulet** showing Thoth as an ibis.*

In his baboon form Thoth wears the moon on his head.

Thutmose III

Four kings of the 18th **Dynasty** were called Thutmose (Tuthmosis). King Thutmose III was only a child when he inherited the throne, so his aunt and stepmother **Hatshepsut** was appointed queen regent. After a few years, Hatshepsut had herself crowned 'king' of Egypt. Thutmose had to be content with being a junior partner for about twenty years. He may have spent this time learning to be a soldier.

A head thought to be Thutmose III.

After Hatshepsut's death Thutmose III tried to copy the military success of his grandfather Thutmose I (see **New Kingdom**) by building up the Egyptian navy and leading the **army** on daring campaigns in Palestine and Syria (see **Warfare**). His greatest victory was a surprise attack on the city of Megiddo. His skill as a general has made historians compare him with the Emperor Napoleon.

Thutmose III won huge amounts of treasure from his enemies during seventeen years of fighting, much of which he spent on building **temples**. He was particularly generous to the temple of **Karnak**, where his victories are recorded on the walls. There are also carvings of many of the unusual plants and animals that the king brought back from his travels, and he may have introduced chickens into Egypt. Thutmose III died in about 1425 BC. His tomb in the **Valley of the Kings** has a **cartouche**-shaped burial chamber decorated with scenes from 'The Book of What is in the Underworld' (see **Underworld Books**).

Time

Egyptian ideas about time were based on watching the cycles of nature – the annual flooding of the Nile, the seasonal habits of plants and animals and the movements of the sun, moon and stars in the heavens. The Egyptian calendar was divided into the three seasons of the farming **year**: the Nile flood, the planting and growth of crops, and the harvest. Days were marked by the rising and setting of the sun, and months by the waxing and waning of the moon.

The Egyptians were also the inventors of the twenty-four-hour clock that we use today. Astronomer-priests watching the night skies from their temple roofs divided the night into twelve hours based on the movements of the circling stars. This was the time when the sun god was believed to be passing through the underworld, and the dangers he faced during each of the twelve hours of night are described in episodes from the **Underworld Books** depicted in royal **tombs**. The day was also divided into twelve hours. Because an hour was a twelfth of the day or night, hours were not always the same length. Daytime hours were longer and night-time hours shorter in the summer, but in winter it was the other way round! The Egyptians could measure the passing of the hours accurately using sundials and water clocks. Water clocks were large **stone** vessels with a small hole in the base that allowed the water inside to escape at a controlled speed. Markings on the side of the vessel made it easy to read the time from the level of the water left inside.

Although star maps showing constellations were painted on the ceilings of some royal tombs, the **zodiac** we know was not introduced until Ptolemaic times (see **Ptolemy**). The Egyptians seem to have had different ideas about earthly and cosmic time, and there were different words for heavenly and earthly eternity. The dead were thought to go on living in their tombs, which were called 'houses of eternity'. As a god the king would of course live forever; in inscriptions he is granted a reign of 'millions of years'.

Papyrus painting of the rising sun. The lions on either side are called Yesterday and Tomorrow.

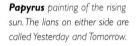

Tomb

The ancient Egyptians thought of tombs as houses for the spirits of the dead. They were the ultimate status symbols for wealthy people. Tombs or tomb-sites could be a gift from the king, but they became the property of the **family** who were buried there. The main tomb-owner was usually the male head of a family but a few important **women** had their own tombs. Sometimes several generations of one family were crammed into the burial chamber. In the **Graeco-Roman Period** it became common to re-use old tombs.

There were two main types of tomb: rock-cut and free-standing (see **Architecture**). In the former, passages and chambers were cut inside a hill. This type of tomb was very common in the limestone cliffs of western **Thebes**. In

free-standing tombs the main part was built above ground in stone or mud-brick (see **Mastaba** and **Pyramids**). The more important the person, the bigger his or her tomb would be. Tombs with carvings or paintings on the walls are known as decorated tombs (see **Art**). Tomb scenes usually show the tomb-owner honouring the gods or enjoying an ideal **afterlife**. About 400 decorated tombs have survived at Thebes.

The actual burial chamber was always underground, even in free-standing tombs. The shaft or passage leading down to the burial chamber was thought of as an entrance to the spirit realm and these underground chambers were sealed up after the burial. So were any rooms where burial goods were stored. Tombs also had one or more rooms where prayers and **offerings** could be made to the spirits of the tomb-owners. These rooms remained open so that **priests** and family members could visit the dead. Some tombs had walled courtyards in front. People used the open areas of family tombs as storerooms, workshops or quiet places.

*The pillared entrance to a rock-cut tomb at **Beni Hasan**.*

*New Kingdom tomb at **Deir el-Medina**, with a miniature pyramid.*

*Free-standing tombs at Tura el-Gebel, the cemetery of **Hermopolis**.*

Tomb robbers

Robbing a tomb in ancient Egypt was a terrible **crime** because taking away the things a dead person needed for the next world denied that person an **afterlife**. If the tomb belonged to a king it was even worse because the king was also a god. Thieves convicted of robbing a royal tomb faced a horrible death. They were either burned alive or impaled on stakes and left to die slowly under the hot sun. Even so, there were plenty of thieves willing to take the risk for the sake of the rich treasures buried with the **kings**. The tomb robbers were very often the same workmen who built the tombs, so they knew exactly how they were laid out and where everything was. One royal tomb at Tanis was burgled by robbers who dug straight through the wall of the burial chamber and into the king's sarcophagus.

Records survive of the trial of several people from **Thebes** accused of robbing royal tombs. This was such a serious case that the **vizier** himself was the chief judge. After being tortured, one man confessed to breaking into a tomb, stealing **jewellery** and **gold**, and burning the royal **mummies** (see **Law and order**). The court took the accused back to the royal tombs and made them point out the ones they had robbed. Surprisingly, some of them were let off – probably because at least one of the judges was involved in the tomb-robbing himself – but the others were executed.

The damaged royal mummies were collected up by the cemetery **priests**, who wrapped them up again and put them in new **coffins** inscribed with their **names**. About forty of them were reburied in a secret hiding place, where they remained undisturbed until a family of modern tomb robbers found them in 1871. These robbers were cleverer. Instead of taking everything at once, they used the mummies as a kind of store, taking a few things at a time and selling them to collectors. The Egyptian authorities knew something was going on but could not find out the truth until, after ten years, one member of the family told on the others. In 1881 the police and army came to take the mummies away to Cairo, where they are now displayed in the Egyptian Museum. People still tell of how, as the **boats** carrying the royal mummies sailed down the Nile, the people from the villages along the river came out to lament their dead pharaohs.

Gold and jasper heart scarab stolen from the mummy of King Sobekemsaf II. The tomb robbers were later caught, forced to confess and executed.

Towns

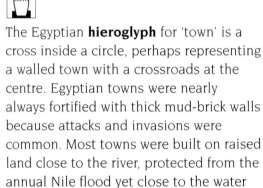

The Egyptian **hieroglyph** for 'town' is a cross inside a circle, perhaps representing a walled town with a crossroads at the centre. Egyptian towns were nearly always fortified with thick mud-brick walls because attacks and invasions were common. Most towns were built on raised land close to the river, protected from the annual Nile flood yet close to the water for transport. The most important building

Hieroglyph meaning 'town'.

The ancient town of Karanis in the Fayum.

in any town was the **temple**, which was also the local administrative centre with offices, stores, **law** courts and sometimes a school and hospital too. The rest of the town was divided into industrial areas and residential districts. In big cities like **Memphis** and **Thebes** there was a royal palace and large villas for the members of the court, but the **houses** of working people were usually crowded together. **Cemeteries** were outside the town in the desert, usually to the west, the direction of the setting sun. From Ptolemaic times, **Alexandria** and other major cities were laid out in **Graeco-Roman** style with broad streets and large public buildings such as theatres and baths.

Toys and games

Board games and counters are among the oldest things recovered from **predynastic** burials, and tomb paintings throughout Egyptian history show people playing board games. The two most popular games were *Mehen* and *Senet*. Mehen was played on a round board carved with a curled-up snake, while Senet was played on a rectangular board divided into squares. People who could not afford special boards played using stones and holes scratched into the ground. Rows of holes carved into the roofs and floors of **temples** may have been for playing a version of Mancala or Wari, an African board game that is still popular today.

Ancient Egyptian children played with very simple toys, which were often home-made. In many cases their designs have changed little over the years: spinning tops of pottery or wood and balls made of cloth or leather stuffed with sawdust or reeds would have been familiar to children 100 years ago. Model people and animals were also popular, and some had moving parts that could be worked with a string. Some children even had little paintboxes.

A couple playing Senet.

Children's toys: balls and a wooden horse with wheels.

A refreshment stand at a local market. The woman stallholder is exchanging two round cheeses for a bag of grain.

Trade

Greek traders were minting coins at Naukratis in the Nile Delta in the 6th century BC, but money was not widely used until the Graeco-Roman Period. Before that, people swapped or 'bartered' things they made or food they grew for the other things they needed. People who worked for the state or private employers were paid in essentials like oil, grain and linen, which they could then exchange for other goods and services. The main trading places were the markets held in towns and villages, but people often made deals between themselves, and there were also travelling salesmen who sailed up and down the Nile or went around visiting homes.

We know quite a lot about Egyptian bartering because sales, especially important ones, were often recorded on scraps of pottery or stone. It was a complicated system because the prices of things depended on what was plentiful or scarce at any one time. Metal kept its value, however, so prices could be fixed against it. Thrifty housewives often spent their spare income on jewellery or metal objects that could be swapped for other things when they were needed, and one clever woman used the profits from her vegetable garden to pay for servants to help her with her work!

Nubian diplomats presenting tribute to the Egyptian king. African trade goods included gold, incense, furs and exotic animals.

International trade was carried out in much the same way. Trading expeditions travelled south to Nubia and Punt laden with goods which they exchanged for things like gold, incense, ebony and ivory, ostrich eggs and feathers, furs and exotic animals. Expeditions were organized by the army. They were difficult and dangerous, and often took a long time – Hatshepsut's trading expedition to Punt was away for three years!

Most expeditions went by water. The ships either had to travel down the Red Sea coast to reach Punt, or sail up the Nile to get to Nubia. Every time they reached one of the Nile cataracts the crew had to get out and drag their craft over the rocks. Overland expeditions travelled through the desert with their goods loaded onto donkeys or carried on the backs of porters. When the traders arrived at their destination they did not always know if the people they met there would be friendly or even speak the same language. Sometimes all the trading had to be done by each side acting out what they wanted!

Trade also played an important part in keeping up friendly relations between Egypt and its Near Eastern and Mediterranean neighbours (see Diplomacy). Egypt's most important exports were linen, papyrus and grain, along with the exotic goods brought from Punt and Nubia. These were exchanged for silver from Syria, copper from Cyprus, olive oil from Crete, cedarwood from Lebanon and lapis lazuli from Afghanistan. Greek traders came to Egypt so often that in the end they were allowed to have their own town at Naukratis in the Nile Delta. A canal linking the Nile with the Red Sea was completed during the Persian period (see Egypt's neighbours), making it easier to trade with Arabia, the source of incense and spices, and perhaps even with far-off India.

Under the Ptolemies regular coinage was introduced, and Alexandria became the main port instead of Memphis.

Aswan remained important as the main market for African produce. During **Roman** times Egypt became the main source of grain for Rome and when the grain ships were delayed by storms, people there went hungry. Alexandria remained the chief port under the Byzantine emperors until the Arabs arrived in the 7th century AD and moved the capital to Cairo.

Travel

The Egyptians were fascinated by **stories** of adventure in foreign lands, although they themselves preferred to stay at home. Foreign travel was associated with exciting activities like **trade**, **warfare** and **diplomacy**, but people had to travel around Egypt on everyday business too.

Most travel was by water and there were many kinds of **boats** for different purposes, from small local ferries to huge sea-going trading ships. Land travel was more difficult. There was not much point in building proper roads because they would just have been washed away each year by the Nile flood. Most people had to walk everywhere unless they were rich enough to be carried about in a sedan chair or could afford a chariot. People did not ride horses and donkeys until late in the **New Kingdom**, and camels were not common before the **Late Period**. Not surprisingly, travel was very slow – it took weeks to get from one end of Egypt to the other and some trading expeditions were away for years.

The Egyptians had always made pilgrimages to holy sites like **Abydos** but travelling for pleasure was unusual before **Greek** and **Roman** times, when visitors began to make special trips to famous monuments like the **Colossi of Memnon**. Classical writers such as the Greek historian Herodotus wrote about their travels in Egypt, adding to its popularity as one of the world's first tourist destinations!

Cargo boat unloading jars of wine.

*Chariots were introduced to Egypt by the Hyksos during the **Second Intermediate Period**.*

Trees

Lots of different kinds of trees grew in the fertile soil of the Nile Valley, providing welcome shade from the hot sun as well as fruit and wood. Fruit trees included dates and figs, and olive trees were planted around **temples** to provide oil for lighting. But good-quality wood was always in short supply. Palm trees were only good for building and most of the other native trees, such as tamarisk, acacia and sycamore, were too small and slow-growing to keep up with demand. This meant that wood was one of Egypt's main imports from the **Old Kingdom** onwards. Cedar and pine were imported from Lebanon, and ebony from Africa. Wood was so precious that Egyptian carpenters were very careful not to waste it and became experts at fitting small pieces together to make large objects like doors, **boats** and **coffins**.

Egyptian trees included the date palm, the sycamore fig and the doum palm.

Tutankhamun

Tutankhamun is one of Egypt's most famous rulers but we do not even know who his parents were. He was probably a son or a much younger brother of the 'Heretic Pharaoh' **Akhenaten**. Tutankhamun was born around 1330 BC and lived for a time in the palace of Queen **Nefertiti** at **Amarna**, although he does not seem to have been her son. He became king when he was only eight or nine years old and was soon married off to one of Akhenaten's teenage daughters by Nefertiti.

Egypt was actually ruled by powerful courtiers such as the **vizier** Ay and a general called Horemheb. They moved the capital back to **Memphis** and reversed all the changes that Akhenaten had made during his reign, repairing the **temples** that Akhenaten had damaged and carving new statues of the **gods**, many of which have the face of the young king. Troops were also sent to impose order among Egypt's subject states.

Little is known about the personal life of Tutankhamun and his **queen**. They seem to have had two children who were stillborn. The king himself died suddenly

*The famous gold mask found on the young king's **mummy** .*

when he was about eighteen years old. Modern examinations of his body suggest that he may have been killed by a blow to the head, which could have been an accident or murder. If it was murder the most likely suspect is the vizier Ay, who unexpectedly became king after Tutankhamun's death. Tutankhamun had probably intended to be buried close to the tomb of **Amenhotep III**, who was either his father or his grandfather, but this tomb was taken over by Ay. Instead the young king was buried in the smallest decorated tomb in the **Valley of the Kings**. Thousands of objects were crammed into his tomb and the king's **mummy** rested inside a solid gold **coffin** and wore a magnificent golden mask.

The entrance to Tutankhamun's burial place was hidden under later building debris, so it survived the **tomb robberies** at the end of the **New Kingdom**. The discovery of the tomb by Howard Carter in 1922 caused a sensation all over the world. Tutankhamun himself made little difference to ancient Egypt, but the treasures from his tomb have inspired hundreds of thousands of people to visit modern Egypt.

Two Ladies

The 'Two Ladies' were two fierce goddesses, Wadjyt and Nekhbet, whose chief role was to defend the sun god and the kings of **Egypt** from their enemies. 'He of the Two Ladies' was one of the titles of an Egyptian king. Wadjyt was linked with Lower Egypt and the Red Crown, and Nekhbet was linked with Upper Egypt and the White Crown (see **Crowns**). Wadjyt was usually a cobra but she could also be shown as a lion-headed woman or as a type of mongoose. Nekhbet was usually a vulture but she was also known as 'the great white cow'.

The pair were sometimes shown as two women or two cobras. Wadjyt usually guarded the king as a cobra (see **Uraeus**), while Nekhbet hovered above him as a vulture. The cobra and the vulture were often painted on temple ceilings and they feature on many pieces of royal **jewellery**. In fact the Two Ladies were probably shown in Egyptian **art** more often than any other deities. If you look for them, you will notice them everywhere.

The Two Ladies painted on a coffin. On the left, Nekhbet as a vulture wearing the White Crown; on the right, Wadjyt as a cobra wearing the Red Crown.

U

Underworld Books

The underworld was the ancient Egyptian realm of the dead and maps of it were painted on some **coffins** of the early 2nd millennium BC. These maps were part of the 'Book of Two Ways', which described in words and pictures two routes to paradise, one by land and one by water.

*A **coffin** with a painted map of the safest routes through the underworld.*

From the 15th to the 12th centuries BC the walls of royal **tombs** were decorated with Underworld Books (see **Valley of the Kings**), which were rather like cartoon-strips because the pictures were just as important as the words. The earliest is 'The Book of What is in the Underworld'. Others have such titles as 'The Book of Caverns', 'The Book of the Earth' and 'The Book of the Divine Cow'. The huge tomb of King Rameses VI has six complete Underworld Books painted on its walls, and scenes from the **Book of the Dead**.

The theme of these books was the journey of the sun god **Ra** through the dark and dangerous world below the earth. The Egyptians believed that the setting sun entered this unseen world each night and that the sun god travelled in a vessel known as 'the Boat of Millions', helped by his crew of powerful deities. The underworld was divided into twelve caverns, one for each of the twelve hours of night (see **Time**). Terrifying demons guarded the entrance to each cavern. During his journey the sun god was attacked by the forces of chaos, led by the serpent **Apophis**. Ra and his companions had to overcome Apophis and the evil spirits known as 'the enemies of Ra'.

As the sun passed through the deepest caverns of the underworld its light brought the dead to life again and the 'enemies of Ra' were defeated and thrown into lakes of fire or boiled alive in cauldrons (see **Crime and punishment**). These gruesome scenes may have influenced Christian ideas of Hell. Each Underworld Book ends with the triumphant rebirth of the sun at dawn. Egyptian **kings** were 'sons of Ra', so their fate was linked to the sun god. They thought that putting the Underworld Books on their tomb walls would help them to be reborn like the sun god. In time most Egyptians came to believe that they would join the sun god in the **afterlife** and fight in the eternal war against the forces of chaos.

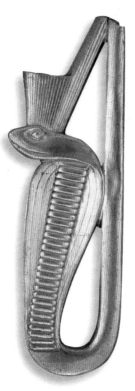

*A **gold** image of the goddess Wadjyt as the uraeus cobra.*

Uraeus

A uraeus was an image of the snake goddess who guarded every Egyptian king. It became a symbol of royalty. The **Greek** word 'uraeus' probably comes from an Egyptian term for a cobra. The image shows a cobra rearing up with her hood spread and her mouth open – the position a female cobra takes to defend her young. The most important cobra goddess was Wadjyt (see **Two Ladies**).

The uraeus was supposed to magically protect the king from his enemies, and many royal **crowns** and headdresses had a uraeus over the centre of the forehead. In some cases the whole body of the cobra is shown coiled across the king's head. Shrines and temple doorways were often topped with a whole row of cobras as a warning to evil forces to keep away.

Ushabti

The ushabti spell from the *Book of the Dead*:
O this shabti, if the Osiris Nebkheperrure [Tutankhamun] is listed for any work that is to be done over there in the underworld, or a tiresome task is put on him there, as part of his duty as a man, you shall say 'Here I am'. If you are listed to serve there at any time, to hoe the fields, to water the river-banks, to carry sand from the east to the west or the west to the east, you shall say 'Here I am!'.

An ushabti or shabti was a special type of figurine that was used in ancient Egyptian burials for about 2,000 years. The earliest ushabtis were meant to act as a spare body if something happened to the tomb-owner's **mummy**. They were usually made of wax and clay, and were stored in miniature **coffins**. Some people buried extra ushabtis in sacred places such as the great **cemetery** at **Abydos**.

Gradually the purpose of these figurines changed. The word 'ushabti' means 'answerer'. In life many Egyptians were called up to carry out manual labour for the state and they were afraid the same might happen in the **afterlife**. The ushabti figurine was supposed to magically answer this summons and do the unpleasant work for them. The spell to make it do so became Chapter Six of the **Book of the Dead** and is often inscribed on the front of the ushabti.

These figurines became such a standard part of the funerary equipment that even **kings** and **sacred animals** were buried with them.

Some ushabti figurines are dressed in everyday **clothes** but most are wrapped like mummies. They often hold **amulets**, sceptres or agricultural tools such as hoes and seedbaskets. Ushabtis were made in **stone**, wood, bronze or **faience**, and some are very beautifully carved or painted. By the **New Kingdom** whole sets of ushabtis were stored in painted wooden chests. Some sets were divided into workers and overseers. King **Tutankhamun** was buried with 365 workers, 48 overseers and 1,866 miniature agricultural tools.

Faience ushabti with matching coffin.

Valley of the Kings

In the **Old Kingdom** most Egyptian kings were buried in **pyramids** in **cemeteries** to the west of **Memphis**, the capital city in northern Egypt. But the problem with pyramids was that they were easy to find and rob (see **Tomb robbers**). **Middle Kingdom** pharaohs began to experiment with other types of tomb. The new ruling families came mainly from **Thebes** in the south and many of them chose to be buried there. There was no space in the narrow Nile Valley to build pyramids, so **tombs** were cut into the high limestone cliffs on the west bank of the river.

At the beginning of the **New Kingdom** King Thutmose I decided that he wanted a new, more secure type of tomb. His architect Ineni later boasted of how he had built the king's tomb in secret, 'nobody seeing and nobody hearing'. The tomb was hidden away in a remote valley in the desert mountains and its entrance was disguised so that once the king was buried no one would be able to find it. Throughout the New Kingdom, Egypt's rulers were buried in the same area, which has become known as the Valley of the Kings. However, they soon stopped trying to conceal their tombs and began to rely on security guards instead.

The Valley of the Kings today, seen from the air. The dark rectangles are the entrances to the ancient royal tombs.

The tombs in the Valley of the Kings consist of a series of halls and corridors going deep into the earth and ending in a burial chamber called the 'House of Gold'. It was here that the pharaoh's body was laid to rest, surrounded by treasure. The walls and ceiling were covered with paintings of **gods and goddesses** who were meant to help the king on his journey through the underworld (see **Underworld Books**). Princes and high officials were also sometimes buried in the valley.

Despite elaborate precautions against looting, nearly all the tombs were robbed in ancient times. Of the sixty-two tombs discovered so far, only that of **Tutankhamun** has been found intact.

Painting in the tomb of King Horemheb in the Valley of the Kings.

Valley of the Queens

The Valley of the Queens, which is a short distance from the **Valley of the Kings** on the west bank of the Nile at **Thebes**, was the main cemetery for royal wives and children during the **New Kingdom**. The tombs are smaller versions of the ones in the Valley of the Kings and their decoration usually shows the tomb-owner being welcomed into the **afterlife** by **gods and goddesses**. The best-known tomb in the Valley of the Queens is that of **Nefertari**, the favourite wife of **Rameses II**, which is famous for its lovely wall paintings. Many of Rameses' sons are also buried in the valley.

Vizier

The vizier, the king's most important **government** minister, was rather like the prime minister in monarchies today. At first there was only one vizier for the whole country, but he had so much work to do that by the **New Kingdom** there had to be two viziers – one for the north of Egypt and one for the south.

The vizier's job was to stand in for the king and oversee all the important affairs of state such as **tax** collection and **building** projects. His official costume consisted of a distinctive long skirt-like garment knotted over the chest and held up by two straps.

When there was no heir to the throne it was not unusual for a vizier, as an experienced and reliable governor, to be chosen as the next king. Both Amenemhet I, founder of the 12th **Dynasty**, and Rameses I, founder of the 19th Dynasty, came to the throne in this way.

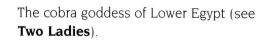

Wadjyt (Wadjet)

The cobra goddess of Lower Egypt (see **Two Ladies**).

Warfare

The Egyptians were basically a peaceful people, but they lived in an unstable part of the world. Ancient Near Eastern rulers were eager to get control of as much territory as possible, so the Egyptians often found themselves at war with their neighbours. Because of invasions from people like the Assyrians, Hyksos, Libyans, Persians and Sea Peoples (see **Egypt's neighbours**), Egypt's borders were guarded by chains of forts and its cities protected by high walls. The Egyptians wanted to control **Nubia** and the **trade** routes between Africa, the Near East and the Mediterranean, because their wealth relied on being able to trade in Nubian **gold** and other important commodities. They preferred to control their empire through **diplomacy**, but when that failed the **army** was always ready to go to war.

Ancient warfare often involved sieges, whereby the invading army surrounded the enemy's city, attacking its walls until the people inside either came out to fight or gave up. When the people in the city were well prepared with food and water supplies, however, they could hold out for a long time. Then the attacking army might run out of supplies itself, or simply get bored and give up. **Rameses II**'s most famous battle, the Battle of Qadesh, ended like this. **Thutmose III**'s general, Djehuty, was

Bronze dagger.

The pharaoh Sety I triumphing over Libyan enemies.

clever: a famous **story** tells how he managed to capture Joppa in Palestine by sneaking 200 soldiers into the city hidden inside baskets!

Unless there was an ambush (which could easily happen in the hilly country around Egypt's borders), armies usually drew up opposite one another on the battlefield and charged when the signal to attack was given. The infantry, armed with spears, swords and daggers, went in first, followed by the chariotry armed with bows and arrows. Most fighting was done hand-to-hand on the ground and there was no mercy. Anything that could be carried was taken, to be shared out after the battle. Captives were brought back to Egypt as **slaves**, and among them were skilled craftsmen such as weavers. New plants and animals were also introduced to Egypt as a result of warfare.

Wedjat Eye

An **amulet** in the form of a falcon's eye (see **Eye of Horus**).

Weighing the heart

A ceremony to judge how a dead person had behaved in his or her life (see **Book of the Dead** and **Scarab**).

Weights and measures

The Egyptians bought and sold things by exchanging goods rather than money (see **Trade**) so it was important to have a good system of weights and measures. The main unit of weight was the *deben* (about 1 kg or 2.2 lb) made up of 10 *kite* (about 100 g or 3.5 oz). These units were mostly used for weighing **metals**, and scenes of goldsmiths' workshops often show precious metals being weighed

Gold rings being weighed on a pair of scales. The weight is shaped like a bull's head.

in scales against animal-shaped weights. The measure of volume used for grain and liquids was called the *hin* and held about half a litre (1 pint). Accurate measurement was so important that **government** officials regularly checked scales and measures and anyone found guilty of cheating was severely punished (see **Crime and punishment**).

The main unit of length was the royal cubit. This was just over 50 cm (20 in) long and was based on the length of a man's forearm. It was divided into seven palm widths, each four fingers wide. The usual cubit measure was a wooden rod marked with these divisions, but **scribes** measuring long distances such as field boundaries used a rope knotted at cubit intervals. The *aroura* (10,000 square cubits) was the unit of land area.

*An official measures a field boundary. The size of a farmer's field determined how much of his crop he would have to give the government in **taxes**.*

Wooden cubit rod.

Wisdom

The ancient Egyptians respected the wisdom of older people, and collections of proverbs and wise sayings were a popular type of literature for over 2,000 years. These collections, which are known as Wisdom or Instruction Texts, are usually in the form of a father advising his son how to behave. The son may argue back but the father always has the last word. Several Instruction Texts claim to be the work of famous people such as **kings**, princes and **viziers**. This probably isn't true, although they were intended for youths who would grow up to be leaders of Egyptian **society**. The advice given covers everything from table manners to ethical issues such as how to treat the disabled. The Egyptians admired people who were calm, patient and kind, and the earliest Wisdom Texts teach young men to avoid anger, greed, injustice and drunkenness.

From the 'Instruction of Anksheshonq', c.300–100 BC:
Don't swear a false oath when you're in trouble, or you'll end up worse off.
Don't ask a god for a guidance and then ignore what he says.
Don't laugh at a cat.

Women

We know the names of some famous Egyptian women like **Hatshepsut** and **Nefertiti**, but they were privileged members of the royal family, not ordinary people. Most women had to take second place to the men of the family, whether they were their fathers, husbands or brothers. As far as the Egyptians were concerned, a woman's place was in the home, and in Egyptian **art** women are often shown with paler skin than men to show that they stayed indoors.

A housewife's daily chores included fetching water, cooking, cleaning, grinding grain, baking bread, brewing beer and washing and mending **clothes**. Some women had vegetable **gardens** to tend and **animals** to care for. Others did spinning and weaving or made clothes. Wealthy housewives could afford plenty of **servants** to help them, and even had maids to do their **hair** and make-up (see **Cosmetics**) for them, but poor women had to do everything themselves.

Some women went to work as servants for others, helping in the house or caring for the **children**. Others worked as musicians, dancers or entertainers (see **Dance** and **Music**). Even though they were not formally educated, women could own their own farms and businesses, and some were very successful. They had their own property and could make wills leaving it to whoever they liked. Some priestesses were also very powerful; during the **Late Period** the God's Wives of Amun effectively ruled the whole of southern Egypt (see **Queens**).

Serving-woman carrying a duck in one hand and a box of beer jars on her head.

Year

The ancient Egyptian calendar was based on the natural cycles of the moon and the river. The year began in the summer with the Nile flood and was divided into three seasons: *Akhet* was the flood season, *Peret* was the growing season and *Shemu* was the harvest season. There were twelve thirty-day months in the year, each divided into three ten-day weeks. This made up 360 days, to which another five days were added at the end of *Shemu*. People thought these extra days were unlucky and called them the 'demon days'. Some Egyptian calendars had unlucky days marked in red and people avoided doing anything important on these days.

Even with the five extra days the Egyptian year was still too short. There was no Leap Year system so the official calendar was usually out of step with the seasons. The **government** used the official calendar anyway, but **temple** calendars were sometimes based on a different system. **Priests** watched the phases of the moon to calculate the right time of year to celebrate religious festivals (see **Time**). The Egyptians dated documents by the year number of the reigning king, which showed how many years he had been on the throne. So a typical date on a letter would read 'Year 12, 2nd month of Peret, Day 5'. When a king died they started again with Year 1 of the new king.

Part of a calendar in the temple of Sobek and Horus at Kom Ombo. The circles and numbers in the left-hand column indicate the days of the month.

Z

Zodiac

The zodiac is a set of twelve astrological signs based on constellations of stars. It originated in Babylon and has been used for fortune-telling from ancient times to the present day. Although the Egyptians knew these constellations, they gave them different names and pictured them in different ways. They did not use the movements of the stars to predict the future, but relied instead on **dreams**, **oracles** and calendars of lucky and unlucky days. From Ptolemaic times (see **Ptolemy**), however, **Greek** and **Roman** ideas began to influence the Egyptians and the zodiac started to appear on **temple** ceilings and **coffin** lids.

A famous zodiac ceiling from the temple of **Hathor** at **Dendera** is now in the Louvre museum in Paris.

Carved zodiac ceiling from the Temple of Hathor at Dendera.

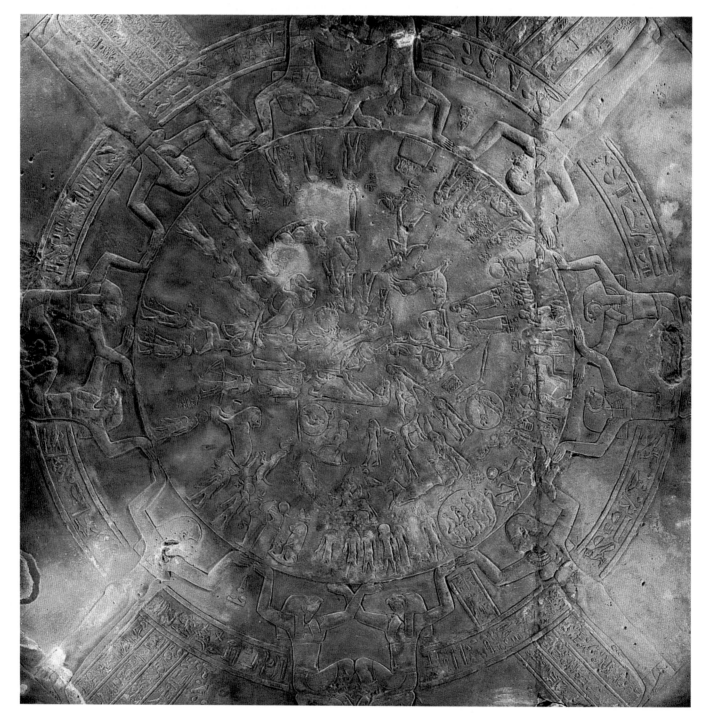

Zoser

King Zoser (Djoser), who ruled Egypt for nineteen years in the 27th century BC, probably fixed the country's southern boundary at **Aswan**. He was the first Egyptian king to build on a gigantic scale. His monument, the Step Pyramid at **Saqqara**, is 62 m (204 ft) high and stands in a great courtyard enclosed by white stone walls. The shrines which surround the **pyramid** are full of details that were copied by later architects. A statue of Zoser, which was walled up in a small chamber, is the earliest known life-size statue of an Egyptian king, and may be the oldest life-size statue of a human being in the world. There is a maze of rooms and tunnels under the pyramid, some decorated with beautiful reliefs and bright turquoise tiles.

The reign of Zoser was remembered for well over 2,000 years. An inscription carved around 200 BC is claimed to be a copy of a decree by him. It describes how Egypt had suffered seven years of famine because the Nile had not risen to water the fields. Zoser ordered his wise minister **Imhotep** to find out who controlled the Nile flood. Imhotep consulted ancient books and discovered that only the ram god **Khnum** could release the Nile from caves hidden deep beneath his temple at Aswan. Zoser hurriedly made rich **offerings** to Khnum. The god came to Zoser in a dream and promised that the Nile would rise high enough to give Egypt plentiful harvests. Zoser decreed that Khnum's temple should be protected and stay wealthy for ever. The inscription ends by warning that anyone who doubts this story will be punished.

The statue of King Zoser from his pyramid complex.

Index

Bold type = Main entry